A
SHORT HISTORY
OF THE
TWELVE JAPANESE BUDDHIST SECTS

A SHORT HISTORY

OF THE

TWELVE JAPANESE BUDDHIST SECTS

TRANSLATED FROM THE ORIGINAL JAPANESE

BUNYIU NANJIO

GYAN

Published by

Gyan Publishing House
5, Ansari Road
Daryaganj, New Delhi-110002
Phone: 011-47034999, 9811692060
E-mail: books@gyanbooks.com

Distribution Network
gyanbooks.com
India, USA, Canada, UK, Australia

ISBN: 978-93-6920-457-1 (HB)

First Published, 1886

2nd Impression 2025

Printed at: Gyan Press, Delhi.

A SHORT HISTORY OF THE TWELVE JAPANESE BUDDHIST SECTS
Author: BUNYIU NANJIO

A SHORT HISTORY

OF THE

TWELVE JAPANESE BUDDHIST SECTS.

RANSLATED FROM THE ORIGINAL JAPANESE

BY

BUNYIU NANJIO, M. A. OXON;

MEMBER OF THE ROYAL ASIATIC SOCIETY, LONDON;
LECTURER ON THE SANSKRIT LANGUAGE
IN THE IMPERIAL UNIVERSITY, TŌKYŌ.

TOKYO:

BUKKYŌ-SHO-EI-YAKU-SHUPPAN-SHA.
MEIJI 19TH YEAR.

CONTENTS.

page

Preface... ... V

Introduction... VIII

Chapter I, the Ku-sha-shū... 1

Chapter II, the Jō-jitsu-shū... 13

Chapter III, the Ris-shū... 20

Chaptor IV, the Hossō-shū... 32

Chapter V, the San-ron-shū... 44

Chapter VI, the Ke gon-shū... 57

Chapter VII, the Ten-dai-shū... ... 68

Chapter VIII, the Shin-gon-shū... 78

Chapter IX, the Jō-do-shū... 104

Chapter X, the Zen-shū... 114

Chapter XI, the Shin-shū... 122

Chapter XII, the Nichi-ren-shū... 132

Sanskrit-Chinese Index... 149

PREFACE.

The aim of the following work is defined by its title; it is a short history, not of Buddhism in general, but of the twelve Japanese Buddhist sects. It is a translation of a Japanese Ms., which consists of an introduction and twelve chapters written separately by nine living Japanese priests within the last seven months. When I was requested by Mr. S. Sano to undertake this work in May last, the Ms. was not yet complete. As my translation was going on, the writers, gradually sent me their respective Ms. from various parts of the country, saying that they wrote in a great hurry. Their style of composition is not always the same, and this has given me a special difficulty to render their words exactly into the English language, with which I am not at all very well acquainted. Moreover the subject itself is of course a very hard one though I have already spent many years in studying it. Whenever the original text is too complicated, I have been obliged to make it short, or to leave certain portions untranslated.

The following are the names of the writers of the text, and some other matters : —

The introduction and the fifth, sixth and eighth chapters on the sects of San-ron, Ke-gon and Shin-gon were written by my friend the Rev. Kō-chō

Ogurusu of the Shin-shū. The first chapter on the Ku-sha-shū was written by the Rev. Shū-zan Emura of the Shin-shū. Another and longer text on the same sect was written by the Rev. Kyoku-ga Saiki of the Shin-gon-shū, but it was too late to be used for this translation. The second and third chapters on the sects of Jō-jitsu and Ritsu are the productions of the Rev. Shō-hen Ueda of the Shin-gon-shū. The writer of the fourth chapter on the Hossō-shū is the Rev. Dai-ryō Takashi of the Shin-gon-shū, and that of the seventh chapter of the Ten-dai-shū is the Rev. Kyō-kwan Uemura of that sect. Another text on the San-ron-shū was written by the Rev. Sō-ken Ueno of the Shin-gon-shū; and that on the Ke-gon-shū, by the Rev. Jitsu-ben Kazuyama of the Ji-shū. But these were also too late to be used for this work. The Revs. Gyō-kai Fukuda, Ken-kō Tsuji, Ren-jō Akamatsu and Ze-jun Kobayashi have each written a chapter on their own sect. Their subjects are the Jō-do-shū (the 9th chapter), the Zen-shū (10th), the Shin-shū (11th) and the Nichi-ren-shū (12th) respectively.

The text is full of proper names and technical terms, which I have mostly restored to their Sanskrit forms, adding the Japanese sound of the Chinese translation or transliteration, and also giving an English translation.

For the orthography of the Sanskrit names and

terms, Professor Max Müller's missionary alphabet has been adopted, as it avoids the use of diacritical marks. It has this peculiarity that italic *k* and *g* are emplyed to represent ch and j as usually pronounced in English. This is because these palatal sounds are derived from gutturals.

For the orthography of the Japanese sound of the Chinese and Japanese names and terms, the alphabet of the Rō-ma-ji-kwai or 'Roman Letter Society' has been adopted.

I greatly regret that the scale of the present work has hindered me from giving in detail the authorities for every statement. In the original text, the authorities are not given, and I have also had no time to look through even the principal books of the tweleve sects, during the progress of this work, as my time has been much occupied by professional duties. Nevertheless I have done my best, though the work be very imperfect indeed.

I have now only most sincerely to thank Dr. W. S. Bigelow for his kindness in correcting some parts of this translation, and Professor Chamberlain for similar assistance with regard to certain others.

Bunyiu Nanjio.

Asakusa, Tōkyō, Japan:

6th December, 19th year of Meiji (1886).

INTRODUCTION.

Those whose minds are confused are called the ignorant. Those whose minds are enlightened are called Buddhas.

Among the confused, there are insects whether flying quickly or moving slowly, such as wasps and caterpillars. There are animals of the scaly tribes, and those covered with shells or crusts. There are animal tribes which are either hairy or naked. Some are one-horned, and others two-horned. Some are two-footed, and others many-footed. Some have wings with which they fly, and others have talons with which they seize their prey. There are large animals called whales; the ferocious are tigers and wolves; the poisonous are vipers and water-bugs; and the cunning are foxes and badgers. There are horned owls which eat their mothers. There are some animals called owl-cats which eat their fathers. Thus there are several different kinds of animals, of which the weeker are always injured by the stronger. Such is the state of the beings who have entered into the nature of animals (Tiryag-yoni-gata, or Chiku-shō-dō, or Bō-shō-shu).

There are Pretas (Ga-ki) or 'departel spirits,' whose bellies are as large as a hill, while their mouths are as small as the eye of a needle; so that they can neither eat nor drink. There are Pretas, for whom water is always changed into fire, as soon as they desire to drink; so that they can never satisfy their thirst. There are Pretas, who eat nothing but excrements and matter. There are Pretas, whose bodies are pierced by their own hairs, the points of which are as sharp as swords. Again there are Pretas, who eat their own children. Such is the state of the Pretas. This state is not seen by human eyes; but among mankind there is often seen something like the above.

The eight hot hells are the states of blazing fire, and the eight cold hells are those of freezing water. The former eight are called Sa*mg*îva (Tō-kwatsu), Kâlasūtra (Koku-jō), Sa*m*ghâta (Shu-gō), Raurava (Kyō-kwan), Mahâ-raurava (Dai-kyō-kwan), Tapana (Shō-netsu), Pratâpana (Dai-shō-netsu), and Avî*k*i (Mu-ken). The latter eight are called Arbuda (A-bu-da), Nirarbuda (Ni-ra-bu-da), A*t*a*t*a (A-se-ta), Apapa (Ko-ko-ba), Hâhâdhara (Ko-ko-ba), Utpala (U-ha-ra), Padma (Ha-do-ma), and Mahâ-padma (Ma-ka-ha-do-ma). No words can sufficiently express the several kinds of sufferings in these hells. Such are the states of the beings in these hells (Nârakas). Both the blazing fire and freezing water are not made by any other being, but by their own thought alone.

Not only the beings who have entered into the

nature of the above three states of the lower animals, departed spirits, and those in the various hells, are confused or perplexed; but also the Devas or heavenly beings, Nâgas or serpents, and the other eight classes of beings (Ten-ryū-hachi-bu) are the same. They are called Mahoragas ('great serpents'), Kinnaras (lit. 'what sort of men?'), Garu*d*as, Râhu ('the seizer'), Asuras, Gandharvas, Râkshasas, Yakshas, Nâgas ('serpents'), Visvakarman ('all-doer'), Sûrya ('the sun'), Soma ('the moon'), Marî*k*i, Mahesvara, *S*akra Devânâm Indra ('the king of gods named *S*akra'), Mahâbrahman, beings of the four Dhyâna-go*k*aras (Shi-zen-ten), and the four Arûpas (Shi-mu-shiki). Though their pains and pleasures are somewhat different from each other, being themselves either holy or ignorant; yet they all belong to the three worlds of desire, form, and formlessness, and are not free from confusion.

Among the beings of the three worlds, men are more thoughtful than all others. Thinking is their mental faculty. Being thoughtful, they are confused. Being thoughtful, they are enlightened, Being thought ful, they become rich and noble. Being thoughtful, they become poor and mean. Being thoughtful, they keep peace. Being thoughtful, they begin to fight. Being thoughtful, they plan to strengthen themselves. Being thoughtful, they fear to be weakened by others. Thus, whether their thinking be skilful or not, some people are flourishing, while others are put to shame.

There are wise princes and clever ministers. There are rebellions ministers and villainous sons. Some people are appointed to high office, given large salaries and intrusted with the power of government. Some people are always picking up things which are rejected or useless. Some dwell in splendid houses and halls, and eat excellent food at every meal. Some live in the dilapidated houses, wear torn clothes, and suffer hunger. Some are in fear of assasins; and others in dread of epidemic disease. Some are in dread of inundation and conflagration; and others are afraid of theives and robbers. Some are drowned in the water, and others are hanged by the neck. There are people either deaf, dumb, or blind. Thus greatly do they differ in happiness and unhappiness; some being joyful, and others sorrowful. This difference depends only on the goodness and badness of their thinking; and they are the effects of the causes of the former existence.

In short, all those who are only careful for the present life and can not see into the future, are called the confused, whether they be wise or ignorant, rich or poor. It is quite impossible for human power to cause every man in the world to become rich and noble, wise and healthy, and long-lived. No religion except the doctrine of Buddha can place all beings in the true state of permanence, joy, self and purity

(Jō-raku-ga-jō, i. e. the four virtues of Nirvâ*n*a). This Buddhism does out of compassion, being itself independent of all the troubles of the three worlds.

Buddha *S*âkyamuni appeared in the world to perform the most important thing, namely, to cause beings to become enlightened. There are many different accounts given of his life. We shall give here an outline of one of these accounts.

LIFE OF BUDDHA.

Buddha was born in the kingdom of Kapila-vastu (Ka-bi-ra-e) in Central India, on the eighth day of the fourth month of the twenty fourth year of the reign of the king Shō of the Shū (Chow) dynasty in China, 1027 B. C. At the moment of his birth, he said: 'I alone, of all beings in heaven above and under the heavens, am worthy of honour.' His father was the Mahâ-râ*g*a or 'great king' *S*uddhodana (Jō-bon Dai-ō), and his mother was the Devî or 'queen' Mâyâ (Maya Bu-nin).

At the age of seven he was thoroughly acquainted with astronomy, geography, arithmetic and military science. At ten he surpassed other princes in shooting through seven iron targets. At fifteen he was formally recognised as heir-apparent. At seventeen he was married to Yasodharâ (Ya-shu-da-ra). At eighteen he began to think of leaving home, because he perceived how existence was traversed by the pains of birth, old age, disease and death. On the seventh day of the second month of his nineteenth year, he entered the forest in order to study the perfect way.

On the seventh day of the second month of his thirtieth year, he awoke to perfect knowledge, while sitting under the Bodhi tree. Buddha had three bodies, viz., 1. Dharma-kâya (Hosshin) or the 'law-body,' which is colourless and formless; 2. Sambhoga-kâya (Hō-shin) or 'the compensation-body,' by which Buddha appears before the Bodhisattvas of the Dasa-bhûmis (Jū-ji) or ten stages; and 3. Nirmâ*n*a-kâya (Ō-jin, or Ke-shin) or the 'transformed body,' by which he appears before the Pratyekabuddhas, *S*râvakas, Devas and men. This is the reason why Buddha *S*âkyamuni was seen differently by the hearers of the Mahâyâna and Hînayâna doctrine during his whole life.

After his enlightenment, Buddha sat for seven days absorbed in meditation, and felt the pleasure of the Law.

In the second week, he preached the Buddhâvata*m*saka-mahâvaipulya-sûtra (Ke-gon-gyō)[1] in nine assemblies held at seven different places. This is called the first period of Ke-gon by Ten-dai Daishi.

On the thirtieth day of the second month (i. e. the

[1] *Nos.* 87,88.

4 th week), Buddha converted the Nâgarâ*g*a or 'snake king' Ma*k*ilinda (Mon-rin Ryū-ō). On the seventh day of the third month, he converted Devapâla (? Dai-i-ha-ri). On the following day, he went to Vârâ*n*asî, where Kau*nd*inya and others were converted. At the age of thirty-one, he converted the Sresh*th*in or wealthy merchant Ya*s*as (Ya-sha Chō-ja). Then he went to the kingdom of Magadha and converted Uruvilvâ-kâ*s*yapa and others. Then, going to Râ*g*ag*ri*ha, he converted King Bimbisâra and his retainers. In the same year, the *S*resh*th*in Kâlya (? Ka-ryō Chō-ja) presented to Buddha the monastery of Ve*n*uvana (Chiku-rin-shō-ja) or the 'bamboo grove.' At the age of thirty-two, he converted Nâgas (Ryū) or snakes and Yakshas (? Ki) or demons, at mount Gaja*s*îrsha (Zō-dzu) or the 'elephant's head.' At thirty-three, *S*âriputra and Mahâmaudgalyâyana became his disciples. At this time the disciples who attained to Arhatship numbered twelve hundred and fifty. In the same year, Mahâkâ*s*yap became a disciple of Buddha. He presented to Buddha a robe valued at one hundred thousand taels. At thirty-four, Buddha was in Vai*s*âli and established the rules of morality. After this year, he constantly added to the number of these rules. At thirty-five, the *S*resh*th*in Sudatta (Shudatsu Chō-ja) of *S*râvastî together with the Prince *G*eta, presented to Buddha the *G*eta-vana Anâtha-

pi*nd*ada-ârâma (Gi-ju Gikko-doku-on) or *G*eta's grove and Anâthapi*nd*ada's garden known as the Gi-on-shō-ja. In this year, Buddha went back to Kapilavastu, when his father King *S*uddhodana sent his retainers and subject people to meet him at a distance of forty miles. The king also selected five hundred rich men to wait upon Buddha, so that he was as splendid as a phoenix flying towards Mount Sumeru. At thirty-six, Buddha preached the Pratyutpanna-buddhasa*m*mukhâvasthita-sûtra (Han-ju-kyō),[2] in Godhanya (Ku-ya-ni). At thirty-seven, Ânanda became his disciple, when he was eight years old. In this year, Buddha converted a younger brother of Kinnara-râ*g*a Druma (Jun Shin-da-ra-ō) on Mount Ryū. At thirty-eight, Râhula became his disciple, when he was nine years old. At thirty-nine, Buddha went to Magadha and converted King Pushya (? Hokka-sha-ō). In this year, a 'votive altar' (Kai-dan) was erected on the south-east of the Gi-on. At forty, Buddha preached to Maitreya (Mi-roku) the Abhinishkrama*n*a-sûtra (Hon-gi-kyō).[3] At forty-one, he returned to Kapilavastu a second time and preached the Buddha-dhyâna-samâdhi-sâgara-sûtra (Kwan-butsu-san-mai-kyō),[4] to his father the king. In this year, his aunt Mahâpra*g*âpatî left home and became a Bhikshu*n*î. During the above twelve years, Buddha spoke for the

[2] *No.* 73. [3] *No.* 509. [4] *No.* 430.

most part the Hînayâna doctrine. This is called the second period of Roku-on (M*ri*ga-dâva or 'deer park') or A-gon (Âgama) by Ten-dai Dai-shi.

At the age of forty two, Buddha preached the Vimala-kîrtti-nirdesa-sûtra (Yui-ma-kitsu-kyō)[5] in the city of Vaisâlî. At forty-three, he preached the Viseshа*k*intâ-brahma-pariprі*kkh*â-sûtra (Shi-yaku-bon-den-sho-mon-gyō).[6] At forty-four, he preached the Laṅkâvatâra-sûtra (Ryō-ga-kyō)[7] on mount Laṅkâ in the Southern sea. In this year he also spoke the Suvar*n*a-prabhâsa-sûtra (Kon-kō-myō-kyō)[8] and the *S*rîmâlâ-devî-si*m*hanâda-sûtra (Shō-man-gyō).[9] From the age of forty-five to forty-nine, Buddha preached the Mahâvaipulya-mahâ-sa*m*nipâta-sûtra (Dai-hō-dō-dai-shikkyō)[10] to Buddhas and Bodhisattvas assembled from ten different regions, by a great stair-case made between the world of desire and that of form. He also preached to Ânanda the *S*ûrâ*m* gama-samâdhi-sûtra (Shu-ryō-gon-gyō).[11] The above eight years are called the third period of Hō-dō (Vaipulya) by Ten-dai Dai-shi.

During the next twenty-two years from the age of fifty to seventy-one, Buddha preached the Pra*gñ*â-pâramitâ-sûtra in sixteen assemblies (Jū-roku-e) held

---

[5] *Nos.* 146,247,149. [6] *Nos.* 189·190. [7] *Nos.* 175, 176,177. [8] *Nos.* 126,127,130. [9] *No.* 59. [10] *No.* 61. [11] *No.* 399.

at four different places, namely, 1. Mount G*ri*dhrakû*t*a ('vulture's peak'), 2. Anâthapi*nd*ada's garden in *S*râvastî, 3. the Abode of the Paranirmitavasavartins (Ta-ke-ji-zai-ten), and 4. the Ve*n*uvana ('bamboo-grove').[12] This is called the fourth period of Han-nya (Pra*gñ*â-pâramitâ) by Ten-dai Dai-shi.

During the last eight years from the age of seventy-

[12] *No.* 1, i. e. the Dai-han-nya-ha-ra-mi-ta-kyō. It is the largest of the Chinese translations of the Buddhist sûtras, as it consists of 600 fasciculi or books. The following is a summary of the contents:—

	FASC.	FASC.	CHAPT.	PLACE OF THE SCENE.
(a)	400	(1–400),	79,	
(b)	78	(401–478),	85,	
(c)	59	(479–537),	31,	G*ri*dhrakû*t*a.
(d)	18	(538–555),	29,	
(e)	10	(556–565),	24,	
(f)	8	(566–573),	17,	
(g)	2	(574–575),		
(h)	1	(576),		*S*râvastî.
(i)	1	(577),		
(j)	1	(578),		Abode of the Paranirmita-vasavartins.
(k)	5	(579–583),		
(l)	5	(584-588),		*S*râvastî.
(m)	1	(589),		
(n)	1	(590),		
(o)	2	(591-592),		G*ri*dhrakû*t*a.
(p)	8	(593-600),		Ve*n*uvana.

one to seventy-nine, Buddha preached for the most part the Saddharma-puṇḍarîka-sûtra (Ho-ke-kyō).[13] He also preached the Amitâyur-dhyâna-sûtra (Kwan-mu-ryō-ju-kyō)[14] to Queen Vaidehî in the city of Râgagriha. At the age of seventy-five, his father the king deid. At seventy-eight, he spoke the Samantabhadra-bodhisattva-karyâ-dharma-sûtra (Fu-gen-bo-satsu-gyō-bō-kyō)[15] in the city of Vaisâlî. At the age of seventy-nine, that was the fifty-first or fifty-third year of King Boku of the Shū (Chow) dynasty in China, 949 B. C., Buddha ascended to the Trayastrimsa heaven (Tō-ri-ten) and preached to his mother Queen Mâyâ.[16] Coming down from it, he preached the Nirvâna-sûtra (Ne-han-gyō)[17] and the Sukhâvatîvyûha (A-mi-da-kyō),[18] etc. At midnight on the fifteenth day of the second month, he entered Parinirvâna, lying down in an avenue of Sâla trees near the city of Kushi. All the Devas and all mankind mourned the departure of their Great Teacher. This is called the fifth period of Hokke and Ne-han by Ten-pai Dai-shi.

Thus we have arranged Buddha's preachings in a chronological order. But this is not at all complete. For the true state of Buddha is not perfectly understood by the Bodhisattvas, Pratyekabuddhas, Srâvakas, Devas and men. The appearance of Buddha in

---

[13] *Nos.* 134. 138. 139. [14] *No.* 198. [15] *No.* 394.
[16] *No.* 153. [17] *Nos.* 113, 114. [18] *No.* 200.

the world is free from any ordinary form and speech. Therefore he can put countless Kalpas in one thought, and make his transformed body appear at several different places at the same time, just as the *K*intâmani (Nyo-i-hō-shu) or fabulous gem yields its possessor all desires, and the sun and moon are reflected in the water of rivers, lakes and wells at one and the same time. In short, Buddha leads those who are not yet enlightened, teaching them the doctrine which he has perfectly understood. The dispositions of beings are various, so that the teachings for them are also divided into several manners. Accordingly there are different classes of doctrines, greater and lesser, partial and complete, temporary and true, apparent and hidden. Though there are numerous doctrine, yet the object is only one, that is, to perceive the truth. If they are confused, all beings on the three worlds are ignorant. If enlightened, the ten different worlds are full of nothing but Buddhas.

BUDDHISM IN INDIA.

There were two schools in India after Buddha's entry into Nirvâ*n*a, namely, 1. the Sthaviras (Jō-za-bu), and 2. the Mahâsa*m*ghikas (Dai-shu-bu). In the former there were five succeeding teachers, whose names are Kâsyapa, Ânanda, Madyhântika, *S*a*n*avâsa and Upagupta. They are equally revered as patriarchs by the followers of the Hînayâna and Mahâyâna schools. In the Ten-daisect, twenty-three patriarchs are ennmerated, with Kâsyapa as the first. Kâsyapa is also the first of the twenty-eight patriarchs of the Zen sect. At the assembly in which Buddha preached the Nirvâ*n*a-sûtra (Ne-han-gyō), Kâsyapa was intrusted with the transmission of the teaching of Buddha's whole life. When the Mahâbrahma-râ*g*a-paripri*kkh*â-sûtra (Dai-bonnō-mon-butsu-ketsu-gi-kyō) was spoken, the secret of the eye of right Law (see chapter 10) was also intrusted to Kâsyapa.

For a hundred years after Buddha, while the five teachers succeed each other as patriarchs, the two schools were harmonious. After that, they began to quarrel. Two centuries after Buddha, the Mahâsa*m*ghikas were divided into nine schools. A century later, the Sthaviras were also divided into eleven schools. These are called the twenty schools of the Hînayâna. Of these, the Sarvâstivâda school was the most flourishing. It depended upon one cheif *S*âstra and on its so-called 'six feet.' The latter are: 1. Sâriputra's Sa*m*gîti-paryâya-pâda(Shū-i-mon-soku-ron),[19] 2. Mahâmaudgalyâyana's Dharma-skandhapâda (Hō-un-soku-ron),[20] 3. Kâtyâyana's (or Mahâmaudgalyâyana's) Pra*gñ*apti-pâda (Shi-setsu-soku-ron),[21] 4. Devasarman's Vi*gñ*âna-kâya-pâda (Shiki-shin-soku ron),[22] 5. Vasumitra's Prakara*n*a-

---

[19] *No.* 1276. [20] *No.* 1396. [21] *No.* 1317. [22] *No.* 1381.

pâda (Hon-rui-soku-ron),[23] and 6. Dhâtu-kâya-pâda (Kai-shin-soku-ron).[24] These six *S*âstras are called the 'six feet,' of which the first three were composed during Buddha's life-time; the fourth was produced a century, and the last two, three centuries after Buddha. The chief *S*âstra is Kâtyâyana's *G*ñâna-prasthâna-*s*âstra (Hot-chi-ron),[25] which also dated from three centuries after Buddha. A century later, five hundred Arhats who were disciples of Kâtyâyana, compiled the Mahâ-vibhâshâ-*s*âstra (Dai-bi-ba-sha-ron).[26] This is a commentary on the last *S*âstra. Nine centuries after Buddha, Vasubandhu (Se-shin) composed the Abhidharma-kosa-*s*âstra (Ku-sha-ron),[27] in which the author sometimes adopts the principles of the Sautrântikas (Kyō-bu). Sa*m*ghabhdra (Shu-gen) then composed the Nyâyânusâra-*s*âstra (Jun-shō-ri-ron)[28] and refuted the last mentioned work. This may show that the flourishing state of the Sarvâstivâda school lasted for some time in India.

Eight hundred and ninety years after Buddha, there was an Indian named Harivarman, who was a disciple of Kumârila-bha*tt*a (?) of the Sarvâstivâda school, and composed the Satya-siddhi-*s*âstra (Jō-jitsu-ron).[29] This book was much studied in India.

The above is an outline of the history of the Hîna-

---

[23] *No.* 1217. [24] *No.* 1282. [25] *No.* 1275. [26] *No.* 1263. [27] *Nos.* 1267, 1269. [28] *No.* 1265. [29] *No.* 1274.

yâna schools in India.

Though the doctrine of the Mahâyâna was transmitted by Kâsyapa and Ânanda, it lost its power, when the doctrine of the Hînayâna became flourishing. Six centuries after Buddha, Asvaghosha (Me-myō) composed the Mahâyâna-sraddhotpâda-sâstra (Dai-jō-ki-shin-ron)[30] and promulgated the Mahâyâna. A century later, Nâgârguna (Ryū-ju) composed the Mahâbhaya-sâstra (Dai-mu-i-ron),[31] the Mahâpragñâ-pâramitâ-sâstra (Dai-chi-do-ron),[32] the Madhyamaka-sâstra (Chū-ron),[33] and other works; with which he explained the apparent doctrine. Finding the iron tower in South India, he also expounded the hidden doctrine.[34] At that time, the Mahâyana school was as bright as the rising sun. Nine centuries after Buddha, Asamga (Mu-jaku) asked the Bodhisattva Maitreya to discourse the Yogâkârya-bhûmi-sâstra (Yu-ga-ron).[35] He himself composed the Mahâyâna-samparigraha-sâstra (Shō-dai-jō-ron),[36] on which his younger brother Vasubandhu (Se-shin) compiled a commentary.[37] The latter also composed the Amitâyus-sûtropadesa (Jō-do-ron),[38] the Buddha-gotra-sâstra (Bus-shō-ron),[39] the Saddharma-pundarîka-sûtra-sâstra (Hokke-ron),[40] the Nirvâna-sâstra

[30] *Nos.* 1249,1250. [31] This has not yet been translated into Chinese. [32] *No.* 1169. [33] *No.* 1179. [34] See Chapter 8. [35] *No.* 1170. [36] *Nos.* 1183,1184. [37] *No.* 1171. [38] *No.* 1204. [39] *No.* 1220. [40] *Nos.* 1232,1233.

(Ne-han-ron),[41] the Va*g*ra*kkh*edikâ sûtra-*s*âstra (Kongō-han-nya-ron),[42] and the Dasabhûmika-*s*âstra (Jū-ji-ron).[43] He also composed thirty verses of the Vidyâmâtra-siddhi-tri-da*s*a-*s*âstra (or-tri*m*sa*kkh*âstra) -kârikâ (Yui-shiki-san-jū-ju),[44] on which ten *S*âstra-teachers each compiled a commentary.[45] The works of Vasubandhu are said to number one thousand in all. The doctrine of the Mahâyâna has become flourishing, owing to the influence of the two teachers Nâgâr*g*una and Vasubandhu. Therefore every Succeeding generation has looked up to them with deep veneration.

BUDDHISM IN CHINA.

In the tenth year of the Ei-hei period, in the reign of the Emperor Mei (Ming) of the Latter Kan (Han) dynasty, 67 A. D., i. e. one thousand and sixteen years after Buddha, the two Indian priests Kâ*s*yapa Mâtaṅga (Ka-shō Ma-tō) and Chiku Hō-ran (Dharmaraksha?) bringing with them an image of Buddha and some sacred books, arrived in Raku-yō, the capital of China. The Emperor then ordered them to live in the Haku-ba-ji, or 'White horse monastery.' This was the first time that Buddhism was known in the Far-East. During the period of the

[41] *No.* 1206. [42] *No.* 1168. [43] *No.* 1194. [44] *No.* 1215.

[45] *No.* 1197, i. e. Jō-yui-shiki-ron, consists of extracts made by the translator Gen-jō from the ten different commentaries.

Latter or Eastern Kan dynasty (25-220 A. D.) and of the San-goku or 'Three Kingdoms' (220-265 A. D.), it was not yet very flourishing. After the Western Shin (Tsin, 265-316 A. D.), or the Eastern Shin (317-420 A. D.), the scholars of the Tripi*t*aka (San-zō-hos-shi) came to China from India one after another, and translated the sacred books into Chinese. From that time, the three trainings in the higher morality, thought and learning became greatly prosperous. China is a vast country and its people are numerous; so that we can not minutely here give the history of Buddhism there, except an outline of the following thirteen sects:—

1. The San-ron-shū, or 'Three *S*âstra sect' (see chapter 5). In 409 A. D., Kumâra*g*îva finished his translation of the Three *S*âstras.[46] His four principal disciples Dō-shō, Sō-jō, Dō-yū and Sō-ei, generally called Shō Jō Yū Ei for brevity, expounded these books. This sect was firmly established by Kichi-zō of the Ka-jō monastery under the Zui (Sui) dynasty, 589-618 A. D.

2. The Jō-jitsu-shū, or 'Satya-siddhi-sâstra-sect' (see chapter 2). Kumâra*g*îva translated the Jō-jitsu-ron,[47] which was extensively taught by the priests of succeeding ages.

3. The Ne-han-shū, or 'Nirvâ*n*a-sûtra-sect.' In 423 A. D., Dharmaraksha (Don-mu-sen) translated

[46] *Nos.* 1179, 1186, 1188. [47] *No.* 1274.

the Ne-han-gyō.[48] E-kwan of the Sō (Sung) dynasty (424–453 A. D.) divided the doctrines into five classes with reference to their chronological order, and called the doctrine of the Nirvâ*n*a-sûtra the fifth doctrine of permanence.

4. The Ji-ron-shū, or 'Da*s*a-bhûmika-*s*âstra-sect.' In 508 A. D., Bodhiru*k*i translated the Jū-ji-ron,[49] which was extensively taught by the priests of succeeding ages.

5. The Jō-do-shū, or 'Pure Land sect' (see chapter 9). Bodhiruki translated the Jō-do-ron or 'Pure Land *S*âstra,' i. e. the Amitâyus-sûtropade*s*a,[50] on which Don-ran of the Gi dynasty (386–534 A. D.) compiled a commentary. At the time of Dō-shaku and Zen-dō (both lived about 600–650 A. D.), this sect was firmly established.

6. The Zen-shū, or 'Dhyâna sect' (see chapter 10). In 520 A. D., the twenty-eighth partriarch Bodhidharma arrived in China, and transmitted the seal of thought to E-ka. It passed throgh Sō-san, Dō-shin and Kō-nin successively. After Kō-nin, the sect was divided into five schools.

7. The Shō-ron-shū, or 'Mahâyâna-sa*m*parigraha-*s*âstra-sect.' In 563 A. D., Paramârtha (Shin-dai) translated the Shō-dai-jō-ron,[51] which was extensively taught by the priests of succeeding ages.

8. The Ten-dai-shū, or 'Mount Ten-dai sect' (see

[48] *No.* 113. [49] *No.* 1194. [50] *No.* 1204. [51] *No.* 1183.

chapter 7). In 551 A. D., E-mon understood the doctrine of Buddha through the Ho-ke-kyō, i. e. Saddharma-pu*nd*arîka-sûtra.[52] He was succeeded by E-shi and Chi-ki. The latter, who is better known by his posthumous title of Chi-sha Dai-shi of Ten-dai (died 597 A. D.), caused this sect to become firmly established.

9. The Ke-gon-shū, or 'Avata*m*saka-sūtra-sect' (see chapter 6). In 418 A. D, Buddhabhadra (Kakugen) translated the Ke-gon-gyō[53] in sixty volumes. Under the Chin dynasty, 557–589 A. D., To Jun expounded it and was succeeded by Chi-gon. At the time of Hō-zō (Gen-ju Dai-shi, died 712 A. D.) this sect was firmly established.

10. The Hossō-shū, or 'Dharma-laksha*n*a sect' (see chapter 4). In 645 A. D., Gen-jō (Hiouen-thsang) returned from India to China and translated many Sūtras and *S*âstras. He bad three thousand disciples; of whom Ki-ki (Ji-on Dai-shi) was the principal one, and who made this sect flourish in China.

11. The Bi-don-shū, or 'Abhidharma-sect' (see chapter 1). In 391 A. D., Gautama Sa*m*ghadeva translated the Hosshō-bi-don, i. e. Abhidharma-h*ri*daya-*s*âstra,[54] which was extensively taught by the priests of succeeding ages. But the flourishing state of this sect dates from the time of Gen-jō (about 650 A. D), when the Ku-sha or Abhidharma-kosa,[55] the

[52] *No.* 134. [53] *No.* 87. [54] *No.* 1288. [55] *No.* 1267.

Ba-sha or Mahâvibhâshâ[56] and other *S*âstras were translated into Chinese.

12. The Kai-ritsu-shū, or 'Vinaya sect' (see chapter 3). In 410 A. D., Buddhayasas translated the Shi-bun-ritsu, or 'Vinaya of four divisions,' i. e. the Dharmagupta-vinaya.[57] There were three great commentators on this book under the Tō (T'ang) dynasty, 618–907 A. D. Among them, Dō-sen of the Nan-zan or Mount Shū-nan is considered the orthodox teacher of this sect.

13. The Shin-gon-shū, or 'Mantra sect' (see chapter 8). In 716 A. D., *S*ubhakarasi*m*ha (Zen-mu-i) arrived in China and greatly promulgated the hidden doctrine. He was succeeded by Va*g*rabodhi (Kon-gō-chi) and Amoghava*g*ra (Fu-kū).

The above thirteen sects are those which existed up to the time of the Tō (T'ang, 618–907 A. D.) and Sō (Sung, 960-1280) dynasties. Since the accession of the Gen (Yuen) dynasty, 1280-1368 A. D, there has been added one sect more, namely, the doctrine of Ra-ma, or Lâmaism, of Tibet. In 1873, I went to Peking, and ascended Mount Go dai (Wu-tai) in the following year. Two years later I visited Mount Ten-dai (Tien-tai), and also went through Sei-ko, Nanking, Bu-shō and Kan-kō. Thus I examined the religions of the people of that vast country, and found out that there were three, viz., 1.

[56] *No.* 1263. [57] *No.* 1117. [58] *Mr.* Ogurusu.

Confucianism (Ju), 2. Buddhism (Butsu), and 3. Taoism (Dō).

There are two great divisions of Buddhism in China at present, namely, the Blue robe sect (Sei-i-ha) and the Yellow robe sect (Kō-i-ha). The Emperor Tai-sō (627-649 A. D.) gave one of his daughters called Bun-sei Kō-shu in marriage to Sampu of To-ban or Tibet. Then the whole of Tibet became a field for Buddhist labourers. Afterwards Sampu frequented India and promulgated the doctrine of Buddha. Lâmaism is a part of the hidden doctrine, and its followers in China form the Yellow robe sect.

The Blue robe sect consists of the priests of the old Chinese sects. They have established the names of Shū or principle, Kyō or teaching, and Ritsu or discipline. The Dhyâna or contemplation is their principle, the doctrines of the Ke-gon or Avata*m*saka-sûtra and the Hokke or Saddharma-pu*nd*arîka-sûtra, etc. are their teachings, and the Vinaya of the Four Divisions or the Dharmagupta-vinaya is their discipline. Therefore each monastery is possessed of these three. The priests in the monasteries on Mount Go-dai belong to the Shō-ryō-shū, i. e. Ke-gon, but they also practise contemplation and discipline. Similarly those on Mount Ten-dai belong to the Chi-sha-shū, i. e. Ten-dai, but they also practise contemplation and discipline. The Chinese

Buddhists seem, therefore, to unite all different sects so as to make one harmonious sect.

BUDDHISM IN JAPAN.

The twelve sects treated of in this book include the principal Japanese Buddhist sects, though the number of different schools might be increased, if we were to count minutely the original and secondary divisions. We shall now try to divide the twelve sects into three periods, namely: —

1. The earliest period includes the first six sects. In the thirteenth year of the reign of the Emperor Kim-mei, 552 A. D., i. e. fifteen hundred years after Buddha, the king of Kudara, one of the three ancient divisions of Korea, presented to the Japanese Court animage of Buddha and some sacred books. In 625 A. D., E-kwan came to Japan from Koma, another division of Korea, and became the founder of the Jō-jitsu and San-ron sects (chapter 2 and 5). At that time, the Prince Imperial Shō-toku (died 621 A. D.) had already promulgated the doctrine of Buddha. In 653 A. D., Dō-shō went to China and studied under Gen-jō and transmitted the doctrine of the Hossō sect to Japan (chap. 4). In 658 A. D., Chi-tsū and Chi-tatsu went to China and also became disciples of Gen-jō and transmitted the doctrines of the Hossō and Ku-sha sects (chaps. 1 and 4). In 703 A. D, Chi-hō and Chi-ran went to China, and so did Gen-bōin 716 A. D. They all transmitted the doctrine of

the Hossō sect. Thus there are four different dates of this transmission. In 736 A. D., a Chinese priest named Dō-sen came to Japan and established the Kegon sect (chap. 6). In 754 A. D., another Chinese priest named Gan-jin arrived in Japan and became the founder of the Ritsu sect (chap. 3). The above may be called the ancient sects, being called the six sects of the Nan-to or Southern Capital, i. e. Nara, where they were established in the earliest period. They are generally enumerated in the order of Ku-sha, Jō-jitsu, Ritsu, Hossō, San-ron and Kegon.

2. The mediæval sects are two, namely, the Ten-dai (chap. 7) and the Shin-gon (chap. 8). These are called the two sects of Kyō-to. In 804 A. D., Saichō and Kū-kai went to China. Having returned to Japan, the former established the Ten-dai sect on Mount Hi-ei; and the latter founded the Shingon sect on mount Kō-ya. In these sects there have been many eminent priests.

3. The modern sects are the remaining four. In 1174 (or 1175) A. D, Gen-kū founded the Jō-do-shū (chap. 9). In 1191 A. D., Ei-sai established the Zen-shū (chap 10). In 1224 A. D., Shin-ran founded the Shin-shū (chap. 11). In 1253 A. D., Nichi-ren founded the Nichi-ren-shū (chap. 12).

It seems to me that as the ancient sects were flourishing in the ancient period only, so were those of the Middle Ages and of modern times in their respective periods. If we want to restore the older sects to their flourishing state, and also to increase the power of the later ones, we must rely on the activity of the determined scholars of all the sects. Is it not true that nations in ancient times were as far from each other as the utmost verge of the heavens or the ends of the earth; so that it was almost impossible to go to and fro? But nations in the present time are not so, as it is very easy to travel through all different countries in a short time, as if the world had become small comparatively.

It is said in the Jō-do-ron, or 'Pure Land *S*âstra:

> 'In any world where there is not known
> The Law of Buddha, which is the pearl of good qualities,
> There I pray that all (Bodhisattvas) shall be born
> And show (the people) the Law of Buddha, just like Buddha himself.'

Must the determined scholars and the men of virtue not examine themselves on this point and become ardent in the pursuit of promulgating the Law?

A SHORT HISTORY OF THE TWELVE JAPANESE BUDDHIST SECTS.

CHAPTER I.

The Ku-sha-shū, or Abhidharma-kosa-sâstra-sect.

1. A history of the sect.

The term Ku-sha is a transliteration of the Sanskrit word Kosa or 'store,' in the title of the principal book of this sect or school, the Abhidharma-kosa-sâstra,'[1] or the 'Book of the treasury of metaphysics.' It was composed by Vasubandhu (Se-shin), who lived in India about nine centuries after Buddha. The *S*âstra is divided into nine chapters, in which the author refers not only to the principal books of the Sarvâstivâdins, one of eighteen schools of the Hînayâna doctrine, but also makes a selection of different views of other schools. The composition is so excellent that it is said to have been praised in India as an 'Intelligence-making *S*âstra' (Sō-mei-ron).

[1] *No.* 1267 in the Min-zō-moku-roku, or Catalogue of the Chinese Translation of the Buddhist Tripi*t*aka, by Bunyiu Nanjio, Oxford, 1883. Similar numbers hereafter refer to those in the same Catalogue.

Although the names of eighteen schools of the Hînayâna are mentioned in the sacred books, yet the doctrines of two of them only are handed down to us at present as subjects of study. These two schools are the Sautrântikas (Kyō-bu) and the Sarvâstivâdins (U-bu). The former is somewhat approximated to by the jō-jitsu-shū, and the latter is represented by the Ku-sha-shū. The character of the Abhidharma-kosa-*s*âstra is, however, very impartial, including the best of all the doctrinal views of the other schools. The doctrine of this *S*âstra is free from inclination to either the peculiar views of the Sarvâstivâdins or those of the Sautrântikas.

The Sarvâstivâdins have many books which belong to the Abhidharma-pi*t*aka (Ron-zō), the last division of the Tripi*t*aka, or the three collections of the sacred books. Among them there are one chief and six secondary works in the following order: —

1. *G*ñâna-prasthâna-sâstra (Hot-chi-ron),[2] by Kâtyâyana. This is the chief book, and the following six works are called the Sha*t*pâda or the 'six feet' of the chief book.

2. Dharma-skandha-pâda (Hō-un-soku-ron),[3] by Mahâmaudgalyâyana.

3. Sa*m*gîti-paryâya-*s*âstra (Shū-i-mon-soku-ron),[4] by *S*âriputra.

4. Vi*g*ñâna-kâya-pâda (Shiki-shin-soku-ron),[5] by

[2] *No.* 1275. [3] *No.* 1296. [4] *No.* 1276.

Devasarman.

5. Pragñapti-pâda (Shi-setsu-soku-ron),[6] by Mahâmaudgalyâyana.

6. Prakarana-pâda (Hon-rui-soku-ron),[7] by Vasumitra.

7. Dhâtu-kâya-pâda (Kai-shin-soku-ron),[8] by the same as before.

Besides these, there is a work entitled Mahâ-vibhâshâ-sâstra (Dai-bi-ba-sha-ron),[9] which was compiled by five hundred Arhats, and is a commentary on Kâtyâyana's *Gñâna*-prasthâna-sâstra.

In 563 A. D. an Indian named Paramârtha (Shin-dai) translated Vasubandhu's *S*âstra into Chinese (A-bi-datsu-ma-ku-sha-shaku-ron),[10] Afterwards, in 654 A. D. under the Tō (T'ang) dynasty, Gen-jō (known as Hiouen-thsang in Europe), made another and better translation (A-bi-datsu-ma-ku-sha-ron).[11] His disciples Fu-kō and Hō-hō each compiled a commentary on the *S*âstra. Besides them, Jin-dai and En-ki also compiled a commentary.

In 658 A. D., two Japanese priests, Chi-tsū and Chi-tatsu, went to China, became disciples of Gen-jō, and brought his new translation of the Kosa or Kusha over to Japan. Thus this *S*âstra was first known in the Empire. Though they did in fact never form an independent sect, being themselves members of

[5] *No.* 1281. [6] *No.* 1317. [7] *No.* 1277. [8] *No.* 1282.
[9] *No.* 1263. [10] *No.* 1269. [11] *No.* 1267.

the Hossō sect, the doctrine taught in the *S*âstra has always been studied by the learners of all the Buddhist sects in Japan till the present day.

II. The doctrine of the sect.

In the Abhidharma-kosa-sâstra, there are many technical terms, such as the five Skandhas (Un) or 'collections,' the twelve Âyatanas (sho) or 'places,' the eighteen Dhâtus (Kai) or 'elements,' and the seventy-five Dharmas (Hō) or 'things.' All these terms are used for explaining things, both Sa*m*sk*ri*ta (U-i) or 'compounded,' and Asa*m*sk*ri*ta (Mu-i) or 'immaterial.' There are also the terms of the four Satyas (Tai) or 'truths,' and the twelve Pratîtya-samutpâdas (En-gi) or 'chains of causation,' and so forth.

Now, let us see what the seventy-five Dharmas are, and how they are grouped together.

1. Sa*m*sk*ri*ta-dharmas (U-i-hō) or 'compounded things.' These are the first seventy-two, the remaining three being Asa*m*sk*ri*ta (Mu-i) or 'immaterial.' The 72 compounded things are grouped under the following four heads.

(1) Rûpas (Shiki) or 'forms,' eleven in number, viz;

1. *K*akshus (Gen) or the 'eye,' that sees;
2. *S*rotra (Ni) or the 'ear,' that hears;
3. Ghrâ*n*a (Bi) or the 'nose,' that smells;
4. *G*ihvâ (Zetsu) or the 'tongue,' that tastes; and

5. Kâya (Shin) or the 'body,' that touches objects.

These five are the Indriyas (Kon) or 'organs of sense,' which have an eminent and vigorous actions

6. Rûpa (Shiki) or 'form,'
7. *S*abda (Shō) or 'sound,'
8. Gandha (Kō) or 'smell,'
9. Rasa (Mi) or 'taste,' and
10. Sparsa (Soku) or 'touch.'

These five are called the Vishayas (Kyō) or 'objects of sense,' on which the organs of sense act.

11. Avi*gñ*apti-rûpa (Mu-hyō-shiki) or 'unapparent form.' This is a peculiar one. Though it is in reality formless, yet it is called form; because its character has some reference to speech and deed, but not to thought. When an action either good or bad is apparent, something will follow it within the actor, which is nevertheless quite unapparent. Hence this object is made distinct.

(2) *K*itta (Shin) or 'mind,' also called Manas (I) or 'thought' and Vi*gñ*âna (Shiki) or 'knowledge.' The Manas is explained by comparison to the pith of a tree, which unites all the branches, leaves, flowers and fruits in one body. If it follows the five organs of sense and thought, it is accounted to be of six kinds. But the *K*itta itself is only one, so that it cannot appear in two or more different places at one

and the same moment. Therefore the Abhidharma-kosa-sâstra speaks of the subject as only one, yet with the names of six different kinds of Vigñâna (Shiki) or 'knowledge,' namely;

1. *K*akshur-vi*g*ñâna (Gen-shiki) or 'eye knowledge,'
2. *S*rotra-vi*g*ñâna (Ni-shiki) or 'ear knowledge,'
3. Ghrâ*n*a-vi*g*ñâna (Bi-shiki) or 'nose knowledge,'
4. *G*ihvâ-vi*g*ñâna (Zetsu-shiki) or 'tongue knowledge,'
5. Kâya-vi*g*ñâna (Shin-shiki) or 'body knowledge,' and
6. Mano-vi*g*ñâna (I-shiki), or 'mind knowledge,'

It is also called the Mano-râ*g*a (Shinnō) or 'mind-king,' because it thinks of every object which appears before it, just as a monarch has the supreme control of every kind of affairs, though the mind or thought itself is also after all one of the seventy-five Dharmas without Âtman or self.

(3) *K*aitta-dharmas (Shin-jo-u-hō) or 'mental qualities.' There are forty-six different qualities, which are again grouped under six heads.

(a) Mahâ-bhûmika-dharmas (Dai-ji-hō) or 'qualities of great ground.' These are ten in number, which always accompany the 'mind' or 'thought.'

1. Vedanâ (Ju) or 'perception,'
2. Sa*m*g*ñ*â (Sō) or 'name,'

3. *K*etanâ (Shi) or 'intention,'
4. Spar*s*a (Soku) or 'touching,'
5. *Kh*anda (Yoku) or 'desire,'
6. Mati (E) or 'intelligence,'
7. Sm*ri*ti (Nen) or 'memory,'
8. Manaskâra (Sa-i) or 'attention,'
9. Adhimoksha (Shō-ge) or 'determination, and
10. Samâdhi (San-ma-ji) or 'self-concentration.'

(b) Ku*s*ala-mahâbhûmika-dharmas (Dai-zen-ji-hō) or 'qualities of great ground of goodness.' There are ten in number, which always accompany the mind when it is good.

1. *S*raddhâ (Shin) or 'calmness of mind,'
2. Apramâda (Fu-hō-itsu) or 'carefulness,'
3. Pra*s*rabdhi (Kyō-an) or 'confidence,'
4. Upekshâ (Sha) or 'equanimity,'
5. Hrî (Zan) or 'shame,'
6. Apatrapâ (Gi) or 'bashfulness,'
7. Alobha (Mu-ton) or 'absence of covetousness,'
8. Advesha (Mu-shin) or 'absence of anger,'
9. Ahi*m*sâ (Fu-gai) or 'not hurting,' and
10. Vîrya (Gon) or 'effort.'

Besides these ten, two more are added in the Vibhâshâ-*s*âstra, namely, wish (Gon) and dislike (En). But, as they do not exist at the same moment, so they are now left out here.

(c) Kle*s*a-mahâbhûmika-dharmas (Dai-bon-nō-ji-hō) or 'qualities of great ground of passions.' There are six in number, which always accompany the mind when it is not pure.

1. Moha (Mu-myō) or 'ignorance,'
2. Pramâda (Hō-itsu) or 'carelessness,'
3. Kausîdya (Ke-dai) or 'indolence,'
4. Asrâddhya (Fu-shin) or 'unbelief,'
5. Styâna (Kon-jin) or 'idleness,' and
6. Auddhatya (Jō-ko) or 'arrogance.'

(d) Akusala-mahâbhûmika-dharmas (Dai-fu-zen-ji-hō) or 'qualities of great ground of badness.' These are two in number, which always accompany the mind when it is not good.

1. Ahrîkatâ (Mu-zan) or 'absence of shame,' and
2. Anapatrapâ (Mu-gi) or 'absence of bashfulness.'

(e) Upaklesa-bhûmika-dharmas (Shō-bon-nō-ji-hō) or 'qualities of ground of secondary passions.' These are ten in number, which do not accompany the mind altogether at one and the same moment like ignorance, etc., but only one after another; so that they are called 'secondary passions.'

1. Krodha (Fun) or 'anger,'
2. Mraksha (Fuku) or 'hypocrisy,'
3. Mâtsarya (Ken) or 'selfishness,'
4. Îrshyâ (Shitsu) or 'envy,'
5. Pradâsa (Nō) or 'vexation,'
6. Vihimsâ (Gai) or 'hurting,'
7. Upanâha (Kon) or 'enmity,'

8. Mâyâ (Ten) or 'deceit,'
9. Sâthya (Ō) or 'dishonesty,' and,
10. Mada (Kyō) or 'vanity.'

(f) Aniyata-bhûmika-dharmas (Fu-jō-ji-hō) or 'qualities of uncertain ground.' These are eight in number, which accompany the mind at any time.

1. Vitarka (Jin) or 'reflection,'
2. Vikâra (Shi) or 'investigation,'
3. Kaukritya (Aku-sa) or 'repentance,'
4. Middha (Sui-men) or 'somnolence,'
5. Râga (Ton) or 'greediness,'
6. Pratigha (Shin) or 'anger,'
7. Mâna (Man) or 'pride,' and
8. Vikikitsâ (Gi) or 'doubt.

The above forty-six are mental qualities (Shin-jo).

(4) Kitta-viprayukta-samskâras (Shin-fu-sō-ō-bō) or 'conceptions separated from the mind.' There are fourteen in all.

1. Prâpti (Toku) or 'attainment,'
2. Aprâpti (Hi-toku) or 'non-attainment,'
3. Sabhâgatâ (Dō-bun) or 'commonness,' i. e. that which makes living beings equal;
4. Asamgñika (Mu-sō-kwa) or 'namelessness,' i. e. the state of one who is born in the Asamgñika heaven, where his mind and mental faculties are in rest during a hundred great kalpas or periods;
5. Asamgñi-samâpatti (Mu-sō-jō) or 'attaininent

of namelessness' by the venerable men,

6. Nirodha-samâpatti (Metsu-jin-jō) or 'attainment of destruction' by the heretics,
7. *G*îvita (Myō-kon) or 'life,'
8. *G*âti (Shō) or 'birth,'
9. Sthiti (Jū) or 'exisetnce,'
10. *G*arâ (I) or 'decay,'
11. Anityatâ (Metsu) or 'non-eternity,' i. e. deat a

The above four (8–11) are called the four forms of the compounded things (Shi-u-i-sō).

12. Nâma-kâya (Myō-shin) or 'name,'
13. Pada-kâya (Ku-shin) or 'word,' and
14. Vyañ*g*ana-kâya (Mon-shin) or 'letter.'

Thus there are seventy-two compounded things, all of which belong to the five Skandhas or collections. The following three complete number of the seventy-five Dharmas explained in the Abhidharma-kosh-*s*âstra. They are not included in the five collections, being immaterial in their nature.

II. Asa*m*skr*i*ta-dharmas (Mu-i-hō) or 'immaterial things.'

1. Pratisa*m*khyâ-nirodha (Chaku-metsu) or 'conscious cessafion of existence.'
2. Apratisa*m*khyâ-nirodha (Hi-chaku-metsu) or 'unconscious cessation of existence.'
3. Âkâ*s*a (Ko-ku) or 'space.'

The above seventy-five Dharmas are, as we have seen, divided into two classes, compounded things and immaterial things. The former include all things that proceed from a cause. This cause is Karma, to which every existing thing is due, Space (Âkâ*s*a) and Nirvâ*n*a (Nirodha) alone excepted. Again, of the three immaterial things, the last two are not subjects to be understood by the wisdom not free from frailty. Therefore the 'conscious cessation of existence' is considered as the goal of all the effort by him who longs for deliverance from misery.

According to the doctrine of the Abhidharma-ko*s*a-*s*âstra, there is a division into three Yânas or vehicles of the *S*râvakas (Shō-mon), Pratyekabuddhas (En-gaku) and Bodhisattvas (Bo-satsu), which help to destroy doubt and make the truth understood. The *S*râvakas meditate on the cause and effect of every thing. If they are acute in understanding, they become free from confusion after three different births. But, if they are dull, they pass sixty kalpas, before they attain to the state of enlightenment. The Pratyekabuddhas meditate on the twelve chains of causation (Jū-ni-innen), or understand the non-eternity of the world, while gazing upon the falling flowers and leaves. Thus they become enlightened, either after passing through four different births, or after a hundred kalpas according to their ability. The Bodhisattvas practise the six Pâramitâs (Roku-do) or 'perfections' and become Buddhas, after three Asa*m*khya or 'countless' kalpas. The six Pâramitâs are the perfect exersice of the same number of principal virtues by a Bodhisattva, as a preliminary to, and indeed a condition of, his attaining Buddhahood. They are as follow: 1. Dâna-pâramitâ, or 'perfect practice of almsgiving,' 2. *S*îla-, or 'morality,' 3. Kshânti-, or 'patience,' 4. Vîrya-, or 'energy,' 5. Dhyâna-, or 'meditation,' and 6. Pra*gñ*â-, or 'wisdom.'

The reason why all things are so minutely explained in this *S*âstra is to drive away the idea of self (Âtman), and to show the truth, in order to make living beings reach Nirvâ*n*a.

Those who may wish to know more of this doctrine, should study the Abhidharma-ko*s*a-*s*âstra, by the help of the two Chinese commentaries of Fu-kō and Hō-hō. After that, they might study the other *S*âstras of the Sarvâstivâdins, which we have already mentioned.

CHAPTER II.

The Jō-jitsu-shū, or Satya-siddhi-*s*âstra-sect.

I. The doctrine of the sect.

The principal book of this sect is entitled the Jō-jistu-ron, or Satya-siddhi-*s*âstra,[1] literally meaning the 'Book of the perfection of the truth.' This book contains selections from and explanations of the true meaning of the Tripi*t*aka, or Three Baskets (San-zō)of the Hînayâna doctrine preached by the Tathâgata. It is the work of an Indian named Harivarman ('lion armour'), a disciple of Kumârila-bha*tt*a (? Ku-ma-ra-da), who was a scholar of the Sarvâstivâda school (U-bu), and lived about nine centuries after Buddha. Harivarman not satisfied with the narrow views of his teacher, made selections of the best and broadest interpretations current in the several different schools of the Hînayâna. Tharefore it is not certain to which school he originally belonged. Some say that it was the Bahu-srutikas (Ta-mon-bu), ohers that it was the Sautrântikas (Kyō-bu). others again say that it was the Dharmaguptas, (Don-mu-toku-bu), or the Mahîsâsakas (Ke-ji-bu). All these different versions are equally without proof. It is therefore better to consider the book indepently as simply eclectic and owning to unite all that was best in each of the Hînayâna schools.

---

[1] *No.* 1274.

Again Ten-dai, Ka-jō and Kumâragîva (Ra-jū) agreed in taking the *S*âstra of this sect as that of the Hînayâna; and Hō-un, Chi-zō and Mon-bin, who were called the three great teachers of the Ryō dynasty (502–557 A. D.), took it as that of the Mahâyâna. These opinions are still one sided. The Vinaya teacher Nan-zan, however, said that the doctrine of the *S*âstra is the Hînayâna, but that its explanations are applicable to the Mahâyâna also. This opinion would perhaps be right. The knowledge of the author of the *S*âstra was so clear, that he was able to explain the deep meaning of the Tripi*t*aka, and express the unreal character of all human knowledge as taught in the Mahâyâna.

What is the best meaning of all the schools of the Hînayâna, selected in the Satya-siddhi-*s*âstra? It is of two kinds of emptiness or unreality, an which as many kinds of meditation are established. The first is the Meditation on emptiness or unreality. As an empty jar, there is not anything to be called Âtman or self in the five Skandhas or collections (which constitute what we should call the consciousness of an intelligent subject). This is therefore the Meditation on the emptiness or unreality of Âtman or self. The second is the Meditation on unselfishness. As the nature of the jar itself is unreal, all things in the five Skandhas are names only. This is the Meditation on Dharmas or things. Thus the two kinds of unreality are explained, so that the meaning of the *Sâstra* are the best of all those of the Hînayâna schools. But as to the way of dispelling doubts for enlightenment, the most minute ones technically known as the Sho-chi-shō, or the 'obstacles of those which are to be known,' or of the want of knowledge, are not removed. Only the obstacles of seeing and thinking, known as the Bon-nō-shō, or the 'obstacles of passions,' are removed. These are the distinctions between the Mahâyâna and Hînayâna.

In the Sarvâstivâda school (U-bu), the Âtman or self is said to be unreal, but the Dharmas or things real. Therefore in the doctrine of that school, the three states of existence are real, and the nature of the Dharmas or things are constantly in existence. But the doctrine of the Satya-siddhi-*sâstra* explains the emptiness of the Âtman and Dharma. It asserts that the past and future are without reality, but the present state of things only stands as if it were real. That is to say, the true state of things is constantly changing, being produced and destroyed each Ksha*n*a (Setsu-na) or 'moment.' Yet it seems as if the state of things were existing, even as a circle of fire seen when a rope-match is turned round very quickly. This is called the 'temporariness continued' (Sō-zoku-ke). Those which are produced by certain causes and combinations of circumstances are called the 'temporariness done by causes' (In-jō-ke). The names of things are made temporarily by the comparison of this and that. This is called the 'temporariness of comparison.' Thus all things are temporary like bubbles, so that they are empty and fleeting. To look upon living beings with the view of the above enumerated three kinds of temporariness is called the 'emptiness of being or self.' This is not the same as the opinion of the Abhidharma school on this subject; because in that school, self is denied on the Skandhas only. Ignorant people and heretics do not know these two kinds of emptiness of the Âtman and Dharma, and have the false idea of seeing and thinking, by which they suffer the misery of transmigration. If one understands the meaning of the two kinds of emptiness, and practises the meditation on them, al his passions will be cured.

This emptiness of the two kinds is not that of nature itself, but that by breaking or destroying the Âtman or self and Dharma or thing. This is one of the differences between the Mahâyâna and the Hînayâna. Again it is said in the *Sâstra* that 'one can obtain enlightenment by one Satya (Tai) or 'truth' only, which is the Nirodha (Metsu), or 'destruction of pain.' This is the third of the four holy truths (Shi-shō-tai). It differs from the views of the Abhidharma school, which says that those of the three Yânas or vehicles of the *S*râvakas, Pratyekabuddhas and Bodhisattvas, see the truth in the same way, and that they attain to the Path by understanding the four truths. Accordingly there are two ways of explaining the title of the Satya-siddhi-sâstra (Jō-jitsu-ron), or 'Book of the perfection of truth:' The first is that it is called so, because it explains perfectly the true meaning of the two kinds of emptiness. The second is that it expounds the reality of the four truths.

This is only an outline of this doctrine.

II. A history of the sect.

According to the Kai-gen-roku,[2] a Catalogue of the Buddhist Books compiled in the Kai-gen period, 730 A. D., Kumâra*g*îva translated the *S*âstra of this school, under the Shin dynasty of the Yō family, in 411-412 A. D. But the Nai-den-roku,[3] another and earlier catalogue, compiled about 667 A. D. puts the date of the translation five years earlier, 406 A. D. The *S*âstra is divided into sixteen or twenty volumes and two hundred and two chapters. When the translation was made, Kumâra*g*îva ordered his disciple Sō-ei to lecture on it; and all his disciples three thousand in number studied and expounded it. In the period of the Sō dynasty, 420-479 A. D., Sō-dō and Dō-kō each compiled a commentary, and the three great teachers already alluded to taught the doctrine of this school under the Ryō dynasty,

[2] *No.* 1485. [3] *No.* 1483.

502-557. Hō-kei compiled another commentary on the *Sâstra* in twenty volumes, under the Chin dynasty, 557-589, and was flourishing under the Zui dynasty, 589-618, and in the earliest period of the Tō dynasty, 618-907. But after Gen-jō's return to China from his famous journey to India, 629-645, the doctrines of the Ku-sha and Ho-ssō schools became more flourishing in China.

Buddhism was first introduced into Japan from Korea in 552 A. D. Thirty years later, the Prince Imperial Shō-toku was born, who, when grown up, became a great promulgator of Buddhism. He studied the doctrines of the San-ron and Jō-jitsu schools, under the instruction of the Korean priests E-ji, E-sō and Kwan-roku. Therefore, in his commentaries on the three Sûtras Saddharma-pu*nd*arîka (Hokke[4]), *Srîmâlâ* (Shō-man[5]), and Vimalakîrtti-nirdesa (Yui-ma[6]), the Prince Imperial depends on the explanations of Kō-taku, who was a teacher of the Jō-jitsu school, and also a promulgator of the Mahâyâna doctrine. In 625, E-kwan came to Japan from Korea. Like Kwan-roku who had already been in Japan, he was a scholar of the San-ron school. Before be left korea for Japan, he went to China and became a pupil of Ka-jō, the founder of that school. The doctrine of the Jō-jitsu school was therefore made known in Japan at the same time as that of the

[4] *No.* 134. [5] *No.* 59. [6] *No.* 146.

San-ron by Kwan-roku and E-kwan. For this reason, the Jō-jitsu school was hereafter always a branch of the San-ron. The scholars of this school always used a great commentary on the *Sâstra* compiled by the Korean priest Dō-zō in sixteen volumes. Besides this there are two other commentaries, the Jō-jitsu-gi-sho in 23 volumes, and the Jō-jitsu-gi-rin in 2 volumes. The reason why the scholars of the San-ron especially studied the Jō-jitsu-ron is this, that Ka-jō, the founder of the San-ron school, constantly refutes the doctrine of the *Sâstra* in his works, in order to make the teaching of the Mahâyâna on emptiness or unreality clear.

The two schools of the Ku-sha and Jō-jitsu have never become independent, the former being a branch of the Hossō, and the latter of the San-ron. Kū-kai, Kō-bō Dai-shi of the Shin-gon sect, said in his last instructions that his followers should study the doctrines of the Hossō and San-ron. If so, they ought also to know the doctrine of the Jō-jitsu. At present, however, the San-ron school is already almost extinct; how much less could the Jō-jitsu school continue to exist? It is hoped that there may be a person, who thinks of this and renews the study of it, in order to understand more clearly the distinctions of the Mahâyâna and Hînayâna.

CHAPTER III.

The Ris-shū, or Vinaya sect.

I. The doctrine of this sect.

This sect was founded by the Chinese priest Dō-sen, Chō-shō Dai-shi, who lived on Mount Shū-nan at the beginning of the T'ang or Tō dynasty (618-907 A.D.). He was well acquainted with the Tripiṭaka, and especially versed in the Vinaya, or discipline. He himself practised the Vinaya, of the Dharmagupta school, according to the Shi-bun-ritsu[1], or Vinaya of Four Divisions, and taught others by it. There is a work entitled Kyō-kai-gi, or 'Rules of Instruction,' written by him for novices. In the preface to it, he says: 'If man does not practise the Dhyâna and Samâdhi (Zen-na and San-mai), i. e. meditation and contemplation, he cannot understand the truth. If he does not keep all the good precepts, he cannot accomplish his excellent practice.' This shows that the wisdom of meditation is produced by keeping the moral precepts.

Moreover the power of Vinaya or precepts also causes the Law of Buddha to exist long in this world. If Buddha's doctrine continues to exist, there will be no calamity in the country, where the people can therefore get salvation. It is the root of all good things. Not only the men of the Hînayâna keep it,

[1] *No.* 1117.

but also those of the mahâyâna do so without any distinction. Accordingly it is called the learning of the Mahâyâna in the *S*rîmâlâ-sûtra (Shō-man-gyō),[2] In the Mahâpra*gñ*â-pâramitâ-*s*âstra (Dai-chi-do-ron),[3] eighty parts (of the Vinaya recited by Upâli on as many occasions in three months of the summer immediately following Buddha's Nirvâ*n*a) are called the *S*îla-pâramitâ, or "perfection of morality.' There is no separate Sa*m*gha, or priesthood, consisting of Bodhisattvas, in the doctrine of *S*âkyamuni. Those who are ignorant of the meaning of the doctrine do notpractise the precepts kept by the Hînayâna, saying that they are men of the Mahâyâna. This is extremely wrong. Dō-sen refuted this view in his works. In the Gō-sho, or 'Work on Action' (Karman), he establishes three doctrinal divisions, viz.

1. The School of True Dharma (Jippō [Jitsu-hō]-shū) i. e. the Sarvâstivâda school, by which Rûpa (Shiki), or form, is considered as the substance of *S*îla, or morality.

2. The School of Temporary Name (Ke-myō-shū), i. e. the Dharmagupta school, by which the substance of the *S*îla is considered neither to be form nor thought. The latter is therefore deeper in meaning than the former.

3. The School of Complete Doctrine (En-gyō-shū),

---

[2] *No.* 59. [3] *No.* 1169.

i. e. the meaning of the two Sûtras Saddharma-pu*n*-*d*arîka.(Hokke)[4] and the Mahâparinirvâ*n*a (Ne-han),[5] by which the temporary vehicle, such as the Hînayâna, is determinately understood as the means to approach the true path. In the two Sûtras above mentioned, the three Yânas or vehicles are admitted, yet they are after all altogether put into one vehicle, i. e. the Mahâyâna. This is technically called Kai-e, literally, 'opening or admitting and uniting.' Dō-sen depended on this principle, and led his disciples to the Complete Doctrine. This is the characteristic of the Vinaya expounded by him, and it is the teaching of the Vinaya sect in Japan.

Although the Dharmagupta-vinaya (Shi-bun-ritsu) of the Hînayâna is used by the sect, the doctrine itself is complete and sudden (En-don) in its character, without any distinction between the larger and smaller vehicles, as well as the three learnings (San-gaku) of morality, meditation and wisdom. It is very high and very deap being the same as the true nature (Jissō) explained in the Saddharma-pu*nd*arîka-sûtra (Hokke),[4] or permanence (Jō-jū) as explained in the Mahâparinirvâ*n*a-sûtra (Ne-han),[5] and the Dharma-dhâtu (Hokkai), or 'state of things,' in the Avata*m*saka-sûtra (Ke-gon).[6]

The Vinaya of all the different schools may equally be said to have the meaning of Kai-e already

---

[4] *No.* 134. [5] *Nos.* 113,114. [6] *Nos.* 87,88.

explained. Why did Dō-sen select the Dharmagupta-vinaya only, in asserting that meaning? Because this Vinaya has been always used by the Chinese Buddhists from olden times. It is the Vinaya of the School of the Temporary Name (Ke-myō), surpassing that of the School of True Dharma (Jippō). Moreover there is a convinience in establishing the doctrine which unites both vehicles, as this Vinaya is equally applicable to the Mahâyana, though it originally belongs to the Hînayâna. For this reason, Dō-sen taught the excellent morality of the one vehicle of completion, without separating it from the Dharmagupta-vinaya.

The three doctrinal divisions above enumerated are made chiefly in connection with morality, but at the same time include the doctrines of meditation and wisdom. Besides these, Dō-sen divided the whole doctrine of the Tathâgata (Nyo-rai, i. e. Buddha) into three parts, namely:

1. The Doctrine of the Emptiness of Nature (Shō-kū-kyō), which includes all the Hînayâna teachings.

2. The Doctrine of the Emptiness of Form (Sō-kū-kyō), which includes all the shallower teachings of the Mahâyâna.

3. The Doctrine of the Completion of the Only Knowledge (Yui-shiki-en-gyō), which includes all the deeper teachings of the Mahâyâna.

These divisions are made in connection with the

doctrines of meditation and wisdom, including the morality taught by Buddha during his whole life.

Now the Vinaya of the Four Divisions (Shi-bun-ritsu) is a part of the Doctrine of the Emptiness of Nature. But Dō-sen judged it from his own thonght as the Doctrine of the Completion of the Only Knowledge, because the three learnings of morality, meditation and wisdom (Kai-jō-e san-gaku) are in fact completly reconciled to each other (Ennyū-mu-ge). Though he made these several divisions, yet he took nothing but completion and quickness as the principle of his doctrine. This is his excellent view.

Moreover, if the learning of *S*îla or morality of the Doctrine of Completion is spoken of with regard to reason, any *S*îla includes the Three Collective Pure *S*îlas (San-ju-jō-kai), viz., 1. the *S*îla of good behaviour, 2. the *S*îla of collecting or holding good deeds, 3. the *S*îla of benevolence towards living beings. But, if it is spoken of with regard to form, there are two ways of receiving it, viz. thoroughly and partially Receiving it thoroughly (Tsū-ju) is to receive the There Collections above enumerated. Receiving it partially (Betsu-ju) is to receive only the first of the Three, viz., the *S*îla of good behaviour. Now the doctrine of *S*îla of Completion in Meaning (En-i-kai) established by Dō-sen, is the latter kind of receiving by a Bodhisattva. In this doctrine, there is an action called Byaku-shi-kom-ma, or Ichi-byakusan-kom-ma, literally, 'once stating (his wish and) thrice (repeating) an action or karman.' That is to say, one who wishes to receive *S*ila has to state his wish bepore a chapter of monks, and then three times he repeats the karmavā*k*ana, or ritual, which his teacher teaches him. After that, he receives the *S*ila of the Bodhisattva. This is what is called 'Receiving thoroughly.'

At present, therefore, the learners of the Vinaya sect prepare both forms of Receiving thoroughly and partially upon the ceremonial platform (Dan-jō), and keep the *S*ila, according to the Vinaya of the Four Divisions (the Hînayâna-vinava) and the Brahma-*g*âla-sûtra (Bon-mō-kyō, i. e. the Mahâyâna-vinaya).[7] The terms 'Receiving thoroughly and partially' originated in the Hossō sect, and they were adopted by Dō-sen in the most active sense. Who could have thus established his doctrine, unless he were a holy person? Boku-sō, an Emperor of the T'ang or Tō dynasty, who reigned from 821 to 824 A. D., praised him with a verse. The Devas and Spiritual Leaders (such as Vai*s*rama*n*a or Bi-sha-mon) are said to have always guarded and praised him and offered him heavenly food; so that if he had a doubt about any thing, the heavenly beings answerd his questions. Last of all, the holy Bhikshu Pindola (Bin-dzu-ru) appeared before

[7] *No.* 1087.

him and praised him, saying that Dō-sen was the best man who had promulgated the Vinaya after Buddha. He is therfore worthy to be honoured and to be believed in by the learners of his doctrine.

II. A history of the sect.

During fifty years, the Tathâgata *S*âkyamuni preached the Vinaya, whenever any circumstance required a rule of discipline After Buddha's entering Nirvâ*n*a, his disciple Upâli, sitting upon a high seat, collected or recited the Vinaya-pi*t*aka, which is called the Vinaya of Eighty Recitations (Hachi-jū-ju-ritsu).[8] In the first century after Buddha, there were five teachers in succession without any different views. Their names are Mahâkâ*s*yapa (Ma-ka-ka-shō), Ânanda (A-nan), Madhyântika (Ma-den-ji), *S*a*n*avâsa (Shō-na-wa-shu), and Upagupta (U-ba-kiku-ta) After the first century, the faithful diverged into two, five, and twenty different schools each possessing the text of the Tripi*t*aka. Among the Vinaya-pi*t*aka of the twenty schools, four Vinayas and five *S*âstras only were transmitted or translated into Chinese. The Vinaya of the Eour Divisions (Shi-bun-ritsu),[9] one of the four Vinayas, is the text of the Dharmagupta school, and has been translated into Chinese in sixty volumes (Kwan). This work was first recited by the Arhat Dharmagupta, one of the five disciples of Upagupta. The

[8] *No.* 1115. [9] *No.* 1117.

names of the five disciples (or rather of their schools) are Dharmagupta (Don-mu-toku), Sarvâstivâda (Sap-pa-ta), Kâsyapîya (Ka-shō-bi), Mahî sâsaka (Mi-sha-soku), and Vâstîputrîya (Ba-so fu-ra).

In the period of the Gi dynasty of the Sō family, 220–265 A. D., Dharmakâla, or Hō-ji, began to teach the Vinaya in China; and in 405, Buddhayasas, or Kaku-myō, first translated the full Vinaya (Shi-bun-ritsu),[10] under the Shin dynasty of the Yō family. These are the dates of the transmission of the Vinaya in China. Sixty years later, there was a Chinese Vinaya-teacher named Hō-sō, who was well acquainted with the Mahâsa*m*ghîka-vinaya (Ma-ka-sō-gi-ritsu).[11] But this Vinaya was not in harmony with that of the Dharmagupta school, which had been adopted in China ever since Dharmakâla; so that he began to teach the Vinaya of the Four Divisions instead of that of the Mahâsa*m*ghikas. From this time down to the Tō (or T'ang) dynasty which lasted from 618 to 907 A. D., the Chinese Buddhists unanimously followed the Vinaya of the Dharmagupta school. This may have been the result of the labours of Hō-sō.

But Dō-sen Nan-zan Dai-shi was the founder of the Vinaya sect in China. Among his works, there are the so called Three Great Books of Vinaya (Ritsu-san-dai-bu), viz., 1. Kai-sho, or Commentary on the Sîla or Morality, in eight volumes; 2. Gossho,

[10] *No.* 1117. [11] *No.* 1119

or Commentary on the Karman or Action, in eight volumes; 3. Gyō-ji-shō, or Record of the Daily Practice, in twelve volumes. There is a catalogue of his works compiled by the Vinaya teacher Gwan-jō.

Dō-sen was succeeded by the second patriarch named Shū, whose successor was Dō-kō. The fifteenth patriarch was Gwan-jō, who was accorded the laudatory name of Dai-chi ('great wisdom'). He was a very learned man, and compiled a commentary on each of the Three Great Books of this sect. Thus the doctrine of Dō-sen was greatly promulgated by him, so that he may be called the re-founder of the Vinaya sect.

Buddhism was introduced into Japan in 552 A. D. But two centuries passed before the doctrine of Vinaya was fully known in this country. In the reign of Shō-mu (724-748), two Japanese priests, Ei-ei and Fu-shō, went to China, and saw the Upâdhyâya (Wa-jō, or Kwa-shō, i. e. teacher) Gan-jin in the Dai-myō monastery of Gō-shū. The latter then consented to their request to promulgate the Vinaya in the East. Gan-jin together with Shō-gen and others eighty in number, promised to come to Japan. They arrived here in 753, having unsuccessfully attempted the journey five times, and having spent twelve years on the sea without approaching Japan. In the following year, the Empress Kō-ken invited him to live in the Eastern Great Monastery (Tō-dai-ji) in Nara, the capital of Japan at that time, and intrusted him with the ordination service, teaching the *S*îla or moral precepts, according to the Vinaya.

Before this, the ex-Emperor Shō-mu, while still on the throne, had by the advice of the venerable Rō-ben, caused a bronze image of Vairo*k*ana Buddha (Bi-ru-sha-na Butsu), the lord of the *S*îla-pâramitâ, or perfection of morality, to be made, one hundred and sixty feet in height, and to be installed in the Eastern Great Monastery. After Gan-jin's arrival, both the ex-Emperor and his daughter, the reigning Empress, took the vow to practise the *S*îla of the Bodhisattvas (Bo-satsu-kai), ascending the Kai-dan, or '*S*îla-terrace,' built of earth before the temple of Vairo*k*ana. The Empress consort and the Prince Imperial as well as many hundreds of priests all followed their example. Afterwards, a separate building of the '*S*îla terrace' (Kai-dan-in) was built to the west of the temple. The earth with which this high terrace was formed, was that which had been used for the terrace of the Emperor; and this earth is said to be that of the *G*eta-vana-vihâra (Gi-on-shō-ja) in India, and of Mount Shū-nan in China. The three stories of the '*S*îla terrace' represent the Three Collective Pure *S*îlas (San-ju-jō-kai). There is placed a tower above it, in which the images of *S*âkyamuni and Prabhûtaratna (Ta-hō) are enshrined; because the excellent meaning of the one vehicle and the deep sense of the secret Dharma-dhâtu are included in this doctrine. Therefore, if one takes the vow to practise the moral precepts on this terrace, he is said to keep the *S*îla of all the hidden and apparent doctrines.

In 759, the Empress Kō-ken ordered Gan-jin to found a monastery called Tō-shō-dai-ji. The '*S*îla terrace' was built therein, where the Empress took the vow. After this, both priests and laymen continually follow her example.

In 762, the following resolution was carried out by Imperial order:— A '*S*îla terrace' was built in two monasteries, Yaku-shi-ji in the province of Shimotsuke and Kwanon-ji in Chiku-zen. The former was the place of taking the vow to practise the *S*îla for the people of the ten eastern provinces; and the latter, for those of the nine western provinces. Both Places, being in remote regions from the capital, a chapter of five monks was held in the ceremony. The people of all the other provinces received instruction in the *S*îla-at the '*S*îla-terrace' within the Eastern Great Monastery in Nara. A chapter of ten monks was regularly held there. There were these three Kai-dan, or '*S*îla terraces,' in Japan. This shows that how greatly the Imperial care was exercise for the sake of the people's religion.

Gan-jin was a successor of two lines of patriarchs, called the lines of Nan-zan and Sō-bu. In the former, he succeeded Gu-kei, who was the successor of Dō-sen, Nan-zan Dai-shi. In the latter, the patriarchs were Hō-rei, Dō-jō, Man-i, Dai-ryō and Gan-jin in succession. Gan-jin was, however, the first patriarch of the Japanese Vinaya sect. He belonged properly to the Nan-zan school, though he was equally a succesor of the Sō-bu; because he received instruction in the full *Sīla* from Gu-kei, who did so from Dō-sen.

CHAPTER IV.

The Hossō shū, or Dharma-lakshana-sect, i. e. the sect or school that studies the nature of Dharmas or things (i. e. the Yoga school).

I. A history of the sect.

The Tathâgata (Nyo-rai) *S*âkyamuni preached the clear meaning of the truth of the 'middle path' of the Vidyâ mâtra (Yui-shiki) or the 'only knowledge'—the principle of the doctrine of this sect—in six Sûtras, such as the Avata*m*saka-sûtra (Ke-gon-gyō),[1] Sandhi-nirmo*k*ana-sûtra (Ge-jin-mitsu-kyō)[2] and others. Nine centuries after Buddha, Maitreya (Mi-roku or Ji-shi) came down from the Tushita heaven to the lecture hall in the kingdom of Ayodhya (A-yu-sha) in Central India, at the request of the Bodhisattva Asa*m*ga (Mu-jaku), and discoursed five *S*âstras (1. Yogâ*k*ârya-bhûmi-*s*âstra (Yu-ga-shi-ji-ron),[3] 2. Vibhâga-yoga (?)-*s*âstra (Fun-betsu-yu-ga-ron),[4] 3. Mahâyânâlaṅkâra-or Sûtrâlaṅkâra-*s*âstra (Dai-jō-shō-gon-ron),[5] 4. Madhyânta-vibhâga-*s*âstra or -grantha (Ben-chū-ben-ron),[6] and 5. Va*g*ra*kkh*edikâ-pra*gñ*âpâramitâ-*s*âstra (Kon-gō han-nya-ron).[7] After that, the two great *S*âstra-teachers Asa*m*ga and Vasubandhu (Se-shin), who were brothers, composed

---

[1] *No.* 87. [2] *No.* 247. [3] 1170. [4] This has not yet been translated into Chinese [5] *No.* 1190 ? [6] *No.* 1244, or *No.* 1245 ? [7] *No.* 1231 ?

many *S*âstras (Ron) and cleared up the meaning of the Mahâyâna. Especially the Vidyâ-mâtra-siddhi-*s*âstra-kârikâ (Jō-yui-shiki-ron)[8] is the last and most careful work of Vasubandhu, as it is perfect in composition and meaning. There were ten great teachers beginning with Dharmapâla (Go-hō), each of whom compiled a commentary. But Dharmapâla's commentary is considered to contain the right meaning of the doctrine. His disciple *S*îlabhadra (Kaigen) lived in the Nâlanda monastery in Magadha in Central India. He was the greatest master of his day, being well versed in the secret meaning of the *S*âstras Yoga and Vidyâ-mâtra (Yui-shiki), as well as in those of the Hetu-vidyâ (In-myō) or 'science of cause,' i. e. the Indian logic or rhetoric, and the *S*abda-vidyâ (Shō-myō) or 'science of sound,' i. e. grammar. This is the history of the doctrine of this sect in India.

In 629 A. D., when he was in his twenty-ninth year, the famous Chinese pilgrim Gen-jō (Hiouen-thsang) went to India and studied the several *S*âstras and Sciences above alluded to, under the instruction of *S*îlabhadra. Having mastered all these subjects, he came back to China in 645. Five months later, he began his great work of translation under the imperial order, in the monastery of Gu-fuku-ji. He continued the work for nineteen years. Thus he

[8] *No.* 1215.

greatly promulgated the doctrine of this sect in China. His principal disciple was Ki-ki, who was very clever and wise. He is said to be the author of a hundred commentaries on several Sûtras and *S*âstras, and was called Ji-on Dai-shi, or the 'great teacher of the Ji-on monastery.' In his works, he generally gives what he had learned by oral instruction from his master Gen-jō. Therefore, most of his works are called Jukki, or 'Records of transmission.' Ki-ki had a disciple named E-shō, (Shi-jū Dai-shi), whose disciple was Chi-shū, (Boku-yō Dai-shi). They each wrote some works and made the doctrine of this sect known in China.

There are four different dates of transmission of this doctrine into Japan, of which the following two dates are clearer and called the Northern and Southern transmission. In 653 A. D., a Japanese priest named Dō-shō of Gwan-gō-ji went to China and became a fellow-disciple of Ki-ki, receiving the instruction from Gen-jō. When he retemed to Japan, he transmitted the doctrine to Gyō-gi. This is the transmission of the so-called Northern monastery, Gwan-gō-ji, being at Asuka in the province of Yamato. Afterwards, in 712 A. D., Gen-bō went to China and studied the doctrine of the Hossō sect, following Chi-shū. Having come back, Gen-bō transmitted it to Zen-ju. This is the transmission of the Northern monastery, Kō-buku-ji, in Nara on the north of Asuka. Since that time, the doctrine has been successively handed down by various learned men.

II. The doctrine of the sect.

(a) The doctrinal division.

According to the Sandhi-nirmo*k*ana-sûtra (Ge-jin-mitsu-kyō), this sect divides the whole preachings of the Tathâgata *S*âkyamuni into the three periods of 'existence' (U), 'emptiness' (Kū), and the 'middle path' (Chū-dō). All the doctrines of the Mahâyâna and Hînayâna, to the number of eighty thousand, are included in these three divisions. In the first period, ignorant people falsely believed in the existence of their own Âtman (Ga) or 'self,' and were accordingly sunk in the sea of transmigration. For such people, the first division of the doctrine of existence was taught by Buddha on purpose, to the effect that every living being was unreal, but that the Dharmas or things were existing. The doctrine preached in the four Âgamas (A-gon)[9] and other Sûtras of the Hînayâna

[9] These are, 1. Madhyamâgama (Ma*gg*hima-nikâya), Chū-a-gon, collection of middle sûtras, *No.* 542.

2. Ekottarâgama (Aṅguttara-nikâya) Zō-ichi-a-gon, miscellaneous Sûtras in divisions the length of which increases by one, *No.* 543.

3. Sa*m*yuktâgama (Sa*m*yutta-nikâya), Zō-a-gon, collection of joined Sûtras, *No.* 544.

4. Dîrghâgama (Dîgha-nikâya), Jō-a-gon, collection of long Sûtras, *No.* 545.

is of this character.

In the second period, though people of small intellect could destroy the false idea of the existence of 'self,' and escape from continual re-births, following the doctrine of the first period; yet they still believed in the 'real existence of Dharmas or things.' Thus they were not able to see the truth. The second division of the doctrine of the 'emptiness of all things was then taught by Buddha still on purpose in the Mahâ-pra*gñ*â-pâramitâ-sûtra and similar works. By this doctrine, the false idea of the 'existence of things' was removed, but it caused man to believe in the 'real emptiness of all things.' Thus there were two kinds of people, one of whom believed in the 'existence or reality of things,' and the other, in the 'emptiness or unreality.'

In order to destroy their false ideas, Buddha in the third period preached the middle path, neither existence nor emptiness, The doctrine of this period shows that the Parikalpita-laksha*n*a (Hen-ge-sho-shū-shō) or the 'invented nature' is unreal, but that the Paratantra-laksha*n*a (E-ta-ki-shō) or the 'subservient nature,' and the Parinishpanna-laksha*n*a (En-jō-jitsu-shō) or the 'completed nature,' are both real. In the Avata*m*saka-sûtra (Ke-gon-gyō) and the Sandhi-nirmo*k*ana-sûtra (Ge-jin-mitsu-kyō), there are given several technical expressions, such as San-gai-yui-shin, or Three worlds (of Kâma [Yoku] or 'desire,' Rûpa

[Shiki] or 'form,' and Arûpa [Mu-shiki] or 'formless') are the only mind; and the eight Vigñânas (Shiki) or 'knowledges,' and the three Lakshaṇas (Shō) or 'natures.'

However, the doctrine is in fact of one and the same tendency, without much difference between the three periods. The human beings are of three classes, viz, those of the highest, those of middle, and those of the lowest intelect, for whom the systems of teaching are necessarily of as many kinds. Those of the highest intellect can understand the true nature of the middle path, which is neither 'existence' nor 'emptiness.' But those of the middle and lowest intellect are unable to understand it at once, only knowing the one side of 'existence' or 'emptiness.' They are called the Bodhisattvas of gradual or slow understanding. At first they know only the existence of things, then the emptiness of them, and finally enter the middle path of 'true emptiness and wonderful existence' (Shin-kū-myō-u).

The three periods are explained in the following two ways. If the three periods are spoken with regard to those of gradual understanding, they are in the order of time. The three words Sho or 'beginning,' Shaku or 'formerly,' and Kon or 'now,' are respectively used for these three periods in the Sandhi-nirmokana-sûtra. But if the division of all teachings of Buddha is made according to the meaning of 'existence, emptiness and the middle path,' then the three periods are the collections of similar meaning: thus the Avata*m*saka-sûtra (Ke-gon-gyō) is put in the third period as it explains the middle path, though it is the first preaching of Buddha; while the Sûtra of the Last Instruction (Yui-kyō-gyō)[10] is included in the first period from its character.

(b) An outline of the doctrine.

This school explains the five ranks or groups of a hundred Dharmas, according to the middle path of the Vidyâ-mâtra-siddhi-*s*âstra (Jō-yui-shiki-ron). They are, 1. *K*itta-râ*g*as (Shinnō) or 'mind-kings,' 2. *K*aitta-dharmas (Shin-jo-hō) or 'mental qualities,' 3. Rûpa-dharmas (Shiki-hō) or 'things having form,' 4. *K*itta-viprayukta-dharmas (Shin-fu-sō-ō-bō) or 'things separated from the mind,' and 5. Asa*m*sk*ri*ta-dharmas (Mu-i-hō) or 'immaterial things.' Though these five groups are enumerated, there is nothing but the *K*itta (Shin) or mind only. There are eight *K*itta-râ*g*as or 'mind-kings,' namely, 1. *K*akshur-vi*gñ*âna (Gen-shiki) or 'eye-knowledge,' 2. *S*rotra-vi*gñ*âna (Ni-shiki) or 'ear-knowledge,' 3. Ghrâ*n*a-vi*gñ*âna (Bi-shiki) or 'nose-knowledge,' 4. *G*ihvâ-vi*gñ*âna (Zetsu-shiki) or 'tongue-knowledge,' 5. Kâya vi*gñ*âna (Shin-shiki) or 'body-knowledge,' 6. Mano-vi*gñ*âna (I-shiki) or 'mind-knowledge,' 7. Klish*t*a-mano-vi*gñ*âna (Zenna-i-shiki or Ma-na-shiki)

[10] *No.* 122.

or 'soiled-mind-knowledge,' and S. Âlaya-vigñâna (A-ra-ya-shiki) or 'receptacle (like)-knowledge.' The eighth has three senses, viz., active (Nō-zō), passive (Sho-zō) and being the object of the false belief (Shū-zō).

In the active sense, it holds the seeds of all things. In the passive, it continues, while receiving the influence of all things. As to the third meaning, it is taken as the inner self or soul by beings. It is called the principal knowledge, because it holds the seeds of all things, which are produced from it accordingly. The first seven kinds of knowledge arise depending upon the eighth. The seventh knowledge takes the 'division of seeing' (Ken-bun) or perception (?) of the eighth as its object. The first five kinds of knowledge take a part of the material world within the 'division of forming' (Sō-bun) or imagination (?) of the eighth as their object. For the sixth, mind-knowledge, all things are its objects.

Therefore all things are made to appear by these eight kinds of knowledge, without which there is nothing whatever. The mental qualities (Shin-jo) are in accordance with, dependent on, and not separated from knowledge. The things that have form (Shiki-hō) are all in the 'division of forms' (Sō-bun) made to appear by the mind and mental qualities, so that they have no separate nature. The 'things separated from the mind' (Shin-fu-sō ō-bō) have no real nature, being formed temporarily upon the part of the mind, mental qualities and forms. The 'immaterial things' (Mu-i-hō) are not any thing made to appear by the mind, being the abstract reason free from birth and death. But they are not separatted from the mind, being the true nature of it. That is to say, things which suffer constant changes of birth and death, or production and destruction, appear according to causes and combination of circumstances; but the abstract reason of the true nature of things itself is permanent and not apparent only. But, if there is no reason, no compounded things ever come to exist. In other words, if there is the reason of production and destruction, then things appear. Therfore Asa*m*skr*i*ta-dharmas, or 'immaterial things,' are those on which Sa*m*skr*i*ta-dharmas, or 'compounded things' depend. Yet they are, of course, not separated from each other, so that the 'only knowledge' (Yui-shiki) includes all compounded and immaterial things.

A hundred Dharmas enumerated in the *S*âstra of this sect are subdivisions of the five ranks as already mentioned. They are the eight *K*itta-râ*g*as, or 'mind-kings,' the fifty-one *K*aitta-dharmas, or 'mental qualities,' the eleven Rûpa-dharmas, or 'things that have form,' the twenty-four *K*itta-viprayukta-dharmas, or 'things separated from the mind,' and the six Asa*m*skr*i*ta-dharmas, or 'immaterial things.' These are the hundred Dharmas of the Vidyâ-mâtra-siddhi-sâstra(Jō-yui-shiki-ron), in which they are also called the two Dharmas of 'matter or thing' (Ji) and 'reason' (Ri). Again, they are altogether inclusively called the 'only mind' (Yui-shin). In the Yoga-sâstra, there are six hundred and sixty Dharmas enumerated.

(c) The doctrine of meditation (Kwan-mon).

In explaining this doctrine, we have to investigate the nature of the object and subject of meditation. In the first place, the object of meditation includes all things compounded and immaterial, and of three different natures. There are five technical expressions on this point, viz.:

1. Ken-ko-zon-jitsu-shiki, or the 'knowledge of rejecting untruth and preserving truth,' is to reject the 'invented nature' (Hen-ge-sho-shū-shō) as emptiness, and to preserve the 'subserveint (E-ta-ki) and completed (En-jō-jitsu) natures' as existing or real.

2. Sha-ran-ru-jun-shiki, or the 'knowledge of rejecting confusedness and preserving pureness,' is to reject objects which may be confused as being both internal and external, and to preserve the mind only that is purely internal.

3. Shō-matsu-ki-hon-shiki, or the 'knowledge of putting away the end, and arriving at the beginning,' is to put away the 'divisions of forming and seeing' (Sō-bun and Ken-bun, i. e. imagination and per-

ception?) as the end, and to arrive at their beginning, the 'division of understanding' (Ji-tai-bun, or Ji-shō-bun).

4. On-retsu-ken-shō-shiki, or the 'knowledge of concealing inferiority and showing superiority,' is to conceal mental qualities (Shin-jo) as inferior to the mind-king (Shinnō) which is superior.

5. Ken-sō-shō-shō-shiki, or the knowledge of rejecting forms and understanding the nature,' is to reject the matters or things (Ji) as forms, and to seek to understand the abstract reason that is the nature. This nature is called the Ji-shō-shō-jō-shin, or 'Self (-existing) natural pure mind,' in the *S*rîmâla-sûtra (Shō-man-gyō). The above five terms explain the object of meditation.

Now the nature of the subject of meditation is Pra*gñ*â (E) or 'wisdom,' one of the mental qualities of a group called the different states' (Betsu-kyō). This is the wisdom which appears in the meditation.

At what time after passing stages and destroying passions, can one who practises the meditation on the 'only knowledge' (Yui-shiki-kwan), attain the state of Buddha? Since first raising his thoughts towards Bodhi or 'enlightenment' deeply and firmly, according to the powers of certain causes and the advice of good friends, he has to pass three great Asa*m*khya or 'countless' kalpas, constantly practising this meditation. Thus, passing through several stages and destroying the two obstacles of passions and cognisable things (Klesa-âvarana and *Gñ*eya-âvarana, or Bon-nō-shō and Sho-chi-shō), he obtains four kinds of wisdom, and truly attains to the perfect enlightenment (Parinirvâna). The fullexplanations of this doctrin are given in the principal *S*âstra of this sect, the Jō-yui-shiki-ron.

CHAPTER V.

The San-ron-shū, or Three *S*âstra sect (i. e. the Madhyamika school).

I. A history of the sect.

The principal books of this sect are three, viz., 1. the Madhyamaka-*s*âstra (Chū-ron) or 'Middle Book,'[1] 2. the *S*ata-*s*âstra (Hyaku-ron) or 'Hundred Books,'[2] and 3. the Dvâda*s*a-nikâya (or-mukha)-*s*âstra (Jū-ni-mon-ron) or 'Book of Twelve Gates.'[3] Hence the name of San-ron-shū. These *S*âstras explain thoroughly the teachings of Buddha's whole life. The sect is therefore, also called Ichi-dai-kyō-shū, or 'Sect of the Teachings of Buddha's Whole Life.' Accordingly it differs much from all other sects which latter are founded on a certain Sûtra or other sacred books. Those who select a Sûtra are liable to become narrow in opinion, and speak about the comparative excellence of other Mahâyâna dectrines; thus the Avata*m*saka-sûtra (Ke-gon-gyō)[4] is regarded by one sect as the principal Sûtra, looking at all the other Sûtras as its branches, while the Saddharma-pu*nd*arîka-sûtra (Ho-ke-kyō)[5] is revered by another sect just in the same way.

This arises from ignorance of Buddha's original thought, which was to make others understand the

[1] *No.* 1179. [2] *No.* 1188. [3] *No.* 1186. [4] *Nos.* 87,88. [5] *No.* 134.

truth. As the dispositions of living beings are of several kinds, the system of teaching for them is also necessarily various. All the doctrines of Mahâyâna have, however, one and the same object without any difference, that is, to cause beings to attain to the middle path. So, any Sûtra or doctrine which suits hearers may be preached to them with advantage. A physician gives his patient a medicine, for the purpose of curing the disease. Who then disputes about the comparative excellence of drugs? The Mahâyâna doctrines are altogether *S*âkya's principal teachings, which are thoroughly explained by the three *S*âstras of this sect.

There are two lines of transmission of the doctrine of this sect, viz., the line of Ka-jō and of Gen-ju.

The former is as follows: The first patriarch in India was the Boddisattva Nâgâr*g*una (Ryū-ju), the author of the Chū-ron and Jū-ni-mon-ron, two of the three *S*âstras. He transmitted the doctrine to the Bodhisattva Deva (Dai-ba), the author of the Hyaku-ron. He was succeeded by Râhula (Ra-gora), whose successor was Nîlanetra (Shō-moku, lit. 'blue eye'). After this, there was a prince of the country of Khara*k*ar (Ki-ji), Sûryasoma by name, who was well versed in the Three *S*âstras and taught the doctrine to Kumâra*g*îva (Ra-jū). In his sixty-third year, Kumâra*g*îva arrived in China, and reached Chō-an, the capital, when he was eighty-one years old. There he translated the Three *S*âstras into Chinese and became the founder of this sect in China. His disciples numbered three thousand, of whom the four greatest (Shi-tetsu) were Dō-shō, Sō-jō, Dō-yū and Sō-ei. Dō-shō transmitted the doctrine to Donsai, Dō-rō, Sō-rō, Hō-rō, and Kichi-zō of the mona-stery of Ka-jō-ji successively. This last named made the doctrine of this sect perfect.

His disciple E-kwan came from Korea to Japan in 625 A. D., and was appointed to Gwan-gō-ji. He once lectured on the Three *S*âstras as prayers to procure rain with success, and was appointed Sō-jō or Bishop. He is considered to be the first patriarch of this sect in Japan. He transmitted the doctrine to Fuku-ryō, who come from Go in China. Fuku-ryō transmitted it to Chi-zō, who went over to China and became a disciple of Kichi-zō, known as Ka-jō Dai-shi. After that, Dō-ji, Zen-gi, Gon-sō and An-chō, etc. successively transmitted this doctrine, and made it flourish in this country.

The other line is that of Nîlanetra (Shō-moku) Bhavaviveka (Shō-ben), *G*ñânaprabha (Chi-kō) and Divâkara (Nichi-shō), who were all Indians. Divâkara transmitted the doctrine to Hō-zō, better known by his posthumous title of Gen-ju Dai-shi, who died in 712 A. D. Af terHō-zō, there was no successor in China.

Of the above two lines of transmission, the Ka-jō

school is considered the orthodox one.

II. The doctrine of the sect.

During his whole life, Buddha preached two kinds of truth (Ni-tai), to remove the confused ideas of the people who were either Astikas, i. e. those who believed in the existence of every thing, or Nâstikas, i. e. those who believed in the emptiness of every thing. These ideas caused them to suffer from endless transmigration, so that they are called the original confusion (Hon-mei). The two kinds of truth are true by general consent (Zoku-tai), and true or absolute truth (Shin-dai). These are not the subjects on which Buddha meditated, but only the differences of the style of his preaching. It is said in the Madhyamaka-*s*âstra, that Buddhas preach the Law to the beings according to the two kinds of truth.

But after Buddha's entry into Nirvâ*n*a, people mistook his words and again became either Astikas or Nâstikas These mistakes are called the later confusion (Matsu-mei). The Three *S*âstras of this sect were then composed by the Bodhisattvas Nâgâr*g*una and Deva, for the purpose of destroying this confusion.

The full title of Chū-ron (Madhyamaka-*s*âstra) is Chū-kwan-ron, or 'Book on the middle meditation.' The word Chū means the middle path of 'not obtaining' (Mu-toku). To contemplate on this middle path is the right meditation. The book contains the words which come out from this right meditation. The words themselves are the two kinds of truth. Truth by general consent (Zoku-tai) is explained for the Nâstikas, who believe that there is nothing. The true truth (Shin-dai) is expounded for the Astikas who believe that there is something. Thus they are equally made to understand the middle path. There are twenty-seven chapters in the Madhyamaka-*s*âstra. The first twenty-five chapters refute the confused ideas of the learners of the Mahâyâna doctrine; and the last two, those of the Hînayâna.

The · Dvâda*s*a-nikâya-*s*âstra (Jū-ni-mon-ron) is divided into twelve parts and refutes the confusion of the men of the Mahâyâna. Generally speaking, this *S*âstra also consists of the words of the two kinds of truth, by which the later confusion is refuted.

The two *S*âstras, Madhyamaka and Dvâda*s*a-nikâya, are the works of Nâgâr*g*una. Did Indians ever believe his works? They did indeed. The people of the sixteen great provinces into which India was formerly divided, unanimously called Nâgâr*g*una 'Buddha without his charactersistic marks' (Mu-sō-gō-butsu), and respected his works as if they had been the Sûtras of Buddha's own words. This respect of the people perhaps originated in the prophecy spoken by Buddha in the Laṅkâvatâra-sûtra (Ryō-ga-kyō),[6] which is as follows:

[6] *Nos.* 175, 176, 177.

'After the Nirvâṇa of the Tathâgata,
There will be a man in the future,
Listen to me carefully, O Mahâmati (Dai-e),
A man who will hold my Law.
In the great country of South,
There will be a venerable Bhikshu,
The Bodhisattva Nâgârjuna by name,
Who will destroy the views of Astikas and Nâstikas,
Who will preach unto men my Yâna ('vehicle'),
The highest Law of the Mahâyâna,
And will attain to the Pramuditâ-bhûmi ('stage of joy'),
And go to be born in the country of Sukhâvatî.'

Now there may be a man who asserts the following opinion. The Laṅkâvatâra is one of the Mahâyâna-sûtras, and these Sûtras are not Buddha's words, but come from the hands of men of later periods. Buddha enterd Nirvâṇa on the fifteenth day of the second month, and two months after, on the fifteenth day of the fourth month, Mahâkâsyapa collected the Tripiṭaka at the Sapta-parṇa ('seven leaves') cave. Besides this collection, there are not any other Sûtras containing Buddha's words. None of the Mahâyâna-sûtras are genuine, so that they are said to have been discovered either in the dragon palace beneath the sea, or in the iron tower in India, etc. Thus they are not worth while to be believed in.

We shall now answer him, so as to make him understand clearly, just as the obstinate clouds are blown away by the strong wind. The Indians who doubted about the genuineness of the Mahâyâna doctrine were of two kinds. Some entertained the doubt, not being free from vulgar and rude customs. The others knew the invincibleness of the Mahâyâna doctrine, yet obstinately uttered these disrespectful words against it.

In ancient times, there were four divisions of people in India (i. e. the four castes). They were 1. Kshatriyas (Setsu-tei-ri), or the royal race, 2. Brâhma*n*as (Ba-ra-mon), or the military class, 3 Vai*s*ya (Bi-sha), or the merchants, and 4. *S*ûdras (Shu-da), or the husbandmen.[7] Besides them, there was a mixed tribe called *K*a*nd*âlas. The men of a higher class looked upon those of a lower, as on the lower animals. For the purpose of destroying this rude custom, Buddha showed them the great path or doctrine, by which they could freely attain to Buddhahood, because they were equally possessed of the nature of enlightenment. But, after Buddha entered Nirvâ*n*a, he people still did not quite forget their old rude

[7] According to the Manu, the four castes are Brâhma*n*as, or the priestly class; Kshatriyas, or the military class; Vai*s*ya, or men whose business was agriculture and trade; and *S*ûdras, or the servile tribe.

customs, and believed only that they might attain to the state of *S*râvakas or Pratyekabuddhas, but not to Buddhahood, which latter would be reached only by a person like *S*âkyamuni in this universe. So that they doubted about the Mahâyâna doctrine, which taught that all beings would become Buddhas. It is just as a Preta (Ga-ki), or departed spirit, cannot see the water but only sees the fire while looking at the real water.

There were three different collections of the Tripi*t*aka made after Buddha's entery into Nirvâ*n*a. The first was the collection made within the cave of seven leaves near Râ*g*ag*ri*ha, the capital of Magadha. This is called the Tripi*t*aka of the Sthavira school (Jō-za-bu). The second was that made without the cave. This is the Tripi*t*aka of the Mahâsa*m*ghika school (Dai-shu-bu). The third was the collection made by Mañ*g*u*s*rî and Maitreya. This is the collection of the Mahâyâna books. Though it is as clear or bright as the sun at midday, yet the men of the Hînayâna are not ashamed at their inability to know them, and speak evil of them instead, just as the Confucianists call Buddhism a law of barbarians, without reading the Buddhist books at all.

There was an event to add some Mahâyâna-sûtras to the Tripi*t*aka of the Hînayâna one hundred and sixteen years after Buddha's Nirvâ*n*a. If there were no Mahâyâna-sûtras, whence were they brought then?

Moreover, two centuries after Buddha, the following Sûtras were also added to the Tripi*t*aka, namely the Avata*m*saka (Ke-gon),[8] Nirvâ*n*a (Ne-han),[9] *S*rîmâlâ-devî-si*m*hanâda (Shō-man),[10] Vimalakîrtti-nirdesa (Yui-ma),[11] Suvar*n*a-prabhâsa(Kon-kō-myō),[12] Pra*g*ñâ-pâramitâ (Han-nya),[13] and others. At that time, neither A*s*vaghosha (Me-myō) nor Nâgâr*g*una (Ryū-ju) was yet born in India. Who can then still say that the Avata*m*saka-sûtra (Ke-gon-gyō) is a work of Nâgâr*g*una?

At that period, the Ekavyahârika school (Ichi-setsu-bu) of the Hînayâna believed in the Mahâyâna doctrine, but the Lokottaravâda school (Shus-se-bu) did not. In the former school, there were perhaps very old men who had heard Buddha's preaching, so that their school was faithful to the Mahâyâna. Two centuries after Buddha's Nirvâ*n*a, Shi-he-e (?) came down from the Himâlaya mountains, and Mahâkâtyâ-yana (Dai-ka-sennen) from the Anavatapta lake (A-nuku-tat-chi). They both were old *S*rama*n*as (Sha-mon), being Buddha's immediate disciples, and somewhat united the Mahâyâna with the Hînayâna. Their schools were called Bahu*s*rutika (Ta-mon) and Bahu*s*rutika-vibha*g*ya (Ta-mon-fun-betsu). It will be seen that some men of the Hînayâna did not abuse the Mahâyâna.

---

[8] *Nos.* 87,88. [9] *Nos.* 113,114. [10] *No.* 59. [11] *Nos.* 146,147,149. [12] *Nos.* 126,127,130. [13] *Nos.* 1–15 *or* 22.

We shall now give a clear proof in order to show the genuineness of the Mahâyâna doctrine from the Mâyâ-sûtra, one of the Hînayâna-sûtras, which are not doubted by the men of the latter school. It reads as follows:—

'The correct Law of the Tathâgata will last for five centuries. In the first century, Upagupta will preach the Law and teach the people. In the second century, the Bhikshu *S*îlananda will do the same. In the third century, the Bhikshu Nîlapadmanetra (Shō-ren-ge-gen, lit. 'blue-lotus-flower-eye') will do so. In the fourth century, the Bhikshu Gomukha (Go-ku, lit. 'cow-mouth') will preach the doctrine. In the fifth century, the Bhikshu Ratnadeva (Hō-ten, lit. 'gem-god') will preach the Law and convert the people to Buddhism. Then the correct Law will come to an end. In the sixth century, heretical views, as many as ninety-six different kinds, will arise and endeavour to destroy the Law of Buddha. But the Bhikshu Asvaghosha (Me-myō) will smash these heretics to atoms. In the seventh century, there will be a Bhikshu named Nâgâr*g*una (Ryū-ju), who will preach the Law with good means, light the torch of the correct Law, and destroy the banner of the unjust views.'

Thus in the Hînayâna-sûtra, Buddha clearly foretold the actions of Nâgâr*g*una seven centuries after him. Who can doubt it? Even an ordinary person is ashamed of making a counterfeit thing. How much less would a great man like Nâgârguna do such a thing? Moreover there is no reason to prophesy a man of such a low character in the sûtras of the both Yânas. After all some Indians perhaps produced a false report, which was then exaggerated by jealous and abusive men. But the true Buddhists do not believe in such a thing.

We shall now examine the origin of the *S*ata-*s*âstra (Hyaku-ron). At the time of the Bodhisattva Deva, a king of South India, who governed many countries, believed in a heretical doctrine and not in Buddhism. Deva said: 'If the root of the tree is not cut off, its branches will not be bent; so, if a king is not converted, the doctrine will not be heard everywhere.' Thus saying, he became a guard of the palace. Holding a spear he commanded the soldiers, regulated the ranks of the army, and made the words of command clear and short. So all the soldiers gladly obeyed him, and the king was very pleased and asked him what to wish to do. Deva said: 'I am a man of all knowing, who want to debate with several scholars of all directions in the presence of Your Majesty.' The king granted his petition. Thereupon Deva caused a high seat to be spread at a cross-road and proposed his theme with the following words:—

'Among all the holy men,

The holy Buddha is the best;
Among all the laws,
The Law of Buddha is the best
Among all those who save the world,
The Buddhist Sa*m*gha (priesthood) is the best.

'If any scholar can overcome these words, I am willing to forfeit my head.'

Then many scholars assembled and Swore saying: 'If we are overcome, we will forfeit our heads.' Deva said: 'The principle of our doctrine is to let the beings live out of compassion, so that we would not want your heads. But if you are overcome, you should shave your heads and become my disciples.'

Thus making an agreement, they began a debate. All the scholars were overcome by Deva, either at once or after two or three days. Three months after, more than a million of people all became his foll-wers. Deva then retired to a forest and recorded what was going on in the debate. This record is the *Sata-sâstra*, which is divided into ten chapters. It refutes chiefly the heretics and sometimes the false belief of the Buddhists also.

If the doctrine of this sect refutes both the Mahâyâna and Hînayâna as well as the heretics, what is the principle of it? Those who keep in mind the difference between our own doctrine and others, and also believe in the variety of the Mahâyâna and Hînayâna, are said to commit errors. The truth is nothing but the state where thoughts come to an end. The right meditation is to perceive this truth. He who has obtained this meditation is called Buddha. This is the doctrine of the San-ron sect.

CHAPTER VI.

The Ke-gon-shū, or Avata*m*saka-sûtra sect.

I. A history of the sect.

(a) The translation of the principal Sûtra.

This sect depends on the Ke-gon-gyō, or Avata*m*saka-sûtra,[1] so that it is called the Ke-gon-shū. There are said to be six different texts of the Sûtra. The first is called the Gō-hon, or 'Constant text,' and the second, the Dai-hon, or 'Great text.' These two texts have been kept by the power of the Dhara*n*î or 'holding' of the great Bodhisattvas, and not written down upon palm-leaves. The third is the Jō-hon, or 'Highest or longest text, and the fourth, the Chū-hon, or 'Middle text.' These two are secretely preserved in the 'dragon palace' (Ryū-gu) under the sea, and not kept by the men of *G*ambudvîpa (En-bu-dai), this world. The fifth is the Ge-hon, or 'Lowest or shortest text,' which is said to contain a hundred thousand verses or as many words in thirty-eight chapters. The Bodhisattva Nâgâr*g*una (Ryū-ju) obtained it from the dragon palace and transmitted it in India.

The sixth is the Ryaku-hon, or the 'Abridged text,' which has been translated into Chinese. Under the Eastern Shin dynasty, 317-420 A. D., Buddhabhadra translated thirty-six thousand verses of the former

[1] *Nos.* 87,88,89.

part of the fifth text in sixty volumes.[2] Afterwards, in the period (695–699) of the Tō (T'ang) dynasty (618–907), *S*ikshânanda translated forty-five thousand verses of the former part of the same text as before in eighty volumes.[3] At the same time, Pra*gñ*a made a separate translation of one chapter entitled Dharma-dhâtvavatâra (Nyū-hō-kai). It consists of forty volumes.[4]

What is the 'Constant text,' that is not to be written down? Even at the point of one grain of dust of immeasurable and unlimited worlds, there are innumerable Buddhas, who are constantly preaching the Ke-gon-gyō, throughout the three states of existence, past, present and future; so that the preaching is not at all to be collected. The one thought of *S*âkyamuni is nothing but the truth (Shin-nyo). This truth fills up all the ten directions throughout the three states of existence. The one thought that is not separated from the truth also fills up the same sphere. While remaining in this one thought, *S*âkyamuni preaches his doctrine, so much so that all things in the ten directions throughout the three states of existence do preach at the same time. Even one Buddha does so. How much more all Buddhas constantly do the same. So, there is no means to collect their preachings completly.

(b) The transmission of the doctrine.

---

[2] *No.* 87. [3] *No.* 88. [4] *No.* 89.

The first patriarch Asvaghosha (Me-myō) composed the Mahâyâna sraddhotpâda-sâstra (Dai-jō-ki-shin-ron),[5] or 'book on raising faith in the Mahâyâna.'

The second patriarch Nâgârguna (Ryū-ju) composed the Mahâ*k*intya-sâstra (Dai-fu-shi-gi-ron), or 'book on the great inconceivableness.' There is now a translation of one part of this book, with the title of Dasabhûmi-vibhâshâ-sâstra (Jū-jū-bi-ba-sha-ron),[6] or 'book on the ten stages fully explained.'

The above two patriarchs were the Indian Bodhisattvas, and the following five were the great Chinese teachers.

The third, To-jun Dai-shi; whose family name was To and his personal name Hō-jun, first established the terms of the 'five doctrines' (Go-kyō), and wrote two works, the Go-kyō-shi-kwan and the Hō-kai-kwan-mon.[7]

The fourth, Shi-sō Dai-shi, whose family name was Chō and his personal name Chi-gon, produced the Sō-gen-ki and the Ku-moku-shō.

The fifth, Gen-ju Dai-shi, whose family name was Kō and his personal name Hōzō, wrote the Go-kyō-sho, Tan-gen-ki, and some other works, and perfected the doctrine of this sect. When he lectured on the sûtra, there rained some wonderful heavenly flowers; and rays of white light came

---

[5] *Nos.* 1249, 1250. [6] *No.* 1180. [7] *No.* 1596.

out from his month. The Empress Soku-ten of the Tō dynasty (reigned 684-705 A. D.) gave him the posthumous title of Gen-ju Bosatsu.

The sixth, Shō-ryō Dai-shi, whose family name was Ka-kō and his personal name Chō-kwan, lived on Mount Go-dai and compiled the Dai-sho-shō,[8] a great commentaly on the Ke-gon-gyō in eighty volumes.

The seventh, Kei-hō Zen-ji, whose family name was Ka and his personal name Shu-mitsu, lived in the Sō-dō monastery on Mount Shū-nan and promulgated the doctrine.

In 136 A. D., a Chinese Vinaya teacher, Dō sen, came to Japan, and first brought the works of this sect. Four years later, Ryō-ben reported to the Emperor Shō-mu, and caused a Korean priest Shin-shō to lecture on the Ke-gon-gyō of sixty volumes, in the Kon-shō ('golden bell') hall of the Tō-dai ji, or the 'Eastern great monastery.' On the opening day, there was seen a cloud of purple colour, which the Emperor admired very much. The lecturer went through twenty volumes a year, and thus completed his task at the end of three yeas. After that, lecturing on the Sûtra has become one of the yearly services of the Tō-dai-ji.

II. The doctrine of the Sect.

(a) The time of Buddha's preaching the

[8] *Nos.* 1589,1890.

Ke-gon-gyō and its title.

After *S*âkyamani attained to Buddhahood, he was silent for seven days. During that period, he meditated on the doctrine which he understood, and also contemplated upon the dispositions of beings, and upon the law to be preached to them. This is called the Sâgara-mudrâ-samâdhi (Kai-in-san-mai), or 'sea-seal-meditation.' As the four troops of the Asuras ('evil spirits') appear upon the great sea, as if it were sealed, so all things including the doctrines and beings appeared upon the wisdom of Buddha, the perfectly enlightened one He preached his doctrine just as it had appeared in the first meditation, but in accordance with the dispositions of hearers. These preachings numbered more than three hundred 'assemblies' or times, which are characterized as the five doctrines of 'smallness (Shō), beginning (Shi), end (Jū), Suddenness (Ton), and completion' (En).

In the second week after his enlightenment, Buddha preached the Ke-gon-gyō, which was therefore the beginning of the preachings of his whole life. This preaching took place at seven different places, where eight assemblies were held, two of which were in the same room. Three of the seven places were in the human world, but the rest in the heavens. It is, however, not to be thought of, that he actually went to so many different places and meetings to discourse. He did not rise from the Jaku-metsu-dō-jō (the place where he became Buddhs), yet he preached in those seven places; because he spoke the doctrine of non-impediment of every thing and endlessness of degrees. Again some might doubt that this Sûtra would not have been preached by Buddha as early as the second week after his attainment; because in the eighth assembly, the *S*râvakas such as *S*âriputra (Sha-ri-hotsu) and Mahâmaudgalyâyana (Dai-moku-ken-ren) who became Buddha's disciples sometime later, were present. But this was done so by the power of the Dhâra*n*î or holding of Buddha. It is said in the Sûtra, that 'all Kalpas of the past are placed in the future, and those of the future are turned to the past.' Therefore it was the power of Buddha's Dhâra*n*î, which caused *S*âriputra and Maudgalyâyana, the later converts, to appear in the assembly of the second week.

The Ke-gon-gyō is the orginal sûtra of Buddha's teachings of his whole life. All his teachings, therefore, sprang from this sûtra. If we attribute, all the branches to the origin, we may say that there is no teaching of Buddha for his whole life, except this sûtra. Now, we shall explain the title of the sûtra in the easiest way, in order to show the outline of the whole work, as the title is said to be a sign of the book. The title of the sûtra in question consists of the seven characters, Dai–hō–kō–butsu–ke-gon–gyō, i. e. Buddhâvata*m*saka (Butsu–ke-gon)-mahâ (Dai)-vaipulya (hō-kō)-sûtra (kyō). The first six characters of Dai-hō-kō-butsu-ke-gon, lit 'great-square-wide-Buddha-flower-adornment,' explain the law taught, and the last Kyō or sûtra means the teaching. Again, among the first six characters, the four of Dai-hō-kō-butsu mean the law or thing compared, while the two of Ke-gon mean a comparison. Among the first four characters, the three of Dai-hō-kō mean the reason understood, and the one of Butsu or Buddha the wisdom of understanding. The whole sûtra is nothing but the reason and wisdom. The reason is Samantabhadra (Fu-gen), and the wisdom, Ma*ñg*usrî (Mon-ju). The state where the reason and wisdom cease to be two, is called Vairo*k*ana's Dharma-kâya (Bi-ru-sha-na-hosshin), or the 'Body of the law of the Great Enlightened,' i. e. Buddha.

The word Dai or 'great' means to contain in; Hō, or 'square,' means rules; Kō or 'wide,' means to extend to. The one and true Dharma-kâya ('law-body') lengthwise contains in it the three states of existence, and crosswise extends to the ten directions. It is free from untruth, so that it is called Dai-hō-kō, 'great-square-wide,' i. e. Mahâ-vaipulya, or 'great largeness.' Buddha understood this truth, by his wisdom and preached it just as he knew. This is the Ke-gon-gyō, or the 'flower-adornment-sûtra,' i. e. Avata*m*saka-sûtra, or 'garland-book.' The Ke-gon or 'garland' is a comparison. The thirty-four chapters preached in the seven places and eight assemblies contain nothing but those in which Buddha became enlightened, just as a garland is made up beautiful by coll cting immeasurably excellent flowers. Therefore the Sûtra is called the Dai-hō-kō-butsu-ke-gon-gyō, i. e. the 'Sûtra of Buddha's garland of great largeness.'

(b) The division of the Five Doctrines (Go-kyō).

As we have seen already, Buddha preached the perfect Sûtra in the second week after his enlightenment. But those of weak intellect, such as *S*âriputra and Maudgalyâyana were like deaf and dumb people, and unable to understand even a word. Accordingly Buddha preached the doctrine of Hînayâna ('small vehicle') with good means. He explained the four truths (Shi-tai) to the *S*râvakas (Shōmon), and the twelve chains of causation (Jū-ni-innen) to the Pratyekabuddhas (En-gaku). He also spoke of a long practice for three Asa*m*khya or 'countless' kalpas to the Bodhisattvas (Bo-satsu) of small intellect. This is only the means of calling in those of weak understanding, just as if it were to make a mirage appear in the space of three hundred Yo*g*anas in order to attract the people to one's own purpose. This is the first of the five doctrines, characterised as 'smallness.'

The second doctrine is described as 'the beginning' (Shi). This is the doctrine which Buddha taught to those who had just entered the Mahâyâna, coming out from the Hînayâna. There are two kinds of this doctrine, namely, that of 'emptiness' (Kū) and of 'form' (Sō). The former (Kū-shi-kyō) is the teaching in which all things are said to be empty or unreal, in order to destroy the false idea of the existence of things (Hō or Dharma) of the Hînayâna. This is the doctrine related in the Pra*gñâ*-sûtra (Han-nya-kyō), the three *S*âstras (San-ron), and similar works. The other (Sō-shi-kyō) is the doctrine which teaches to practise disciplines profitable both for oneself and others, for attaining to Buddhahood. It increases the six kinds of Vi*gñ*âna or knowledge of the Hînayâna into eight, and also the seventy-five Dharmas into a hundred. (For these, see Chapters 1 and 4, i. e. the Ku-sha-shū and Hossō-shū.) This is the doctrine of the Sandhi-nirmo*k*ana-sûtra (Ge-jin-mitsu-kyō), the Yogâ*k*ârya-bhûmi-sâstra (Yu-ga-ron), and the like.

The third doctrine is called 'the end' (Jū), that is to say, the extremity of the Mahâyâna. This doctrine speaks of the causation from the Tathâgata-garbha (Nyo-rai-zō) or the 'Tathâgata's womb;' but not of the Bhûta-tathatâ (Shin-nyo) or the 'true suchness' or truth. It also asserts that all can become Buddhas but not that men are of five different kinds in their nature (the latter views being those of the Hossō sect). It is the doctrine that is expounded in the Laṅkâvatâra-sûtra (Ryō-ga-kyō),[9] the Mahâyâna-sraddhotpâda-sâstra (Ki-shin-ron), and other works.

The fourth doctrine is characterised as 'Suddenness.' It teaches that when a thought does not rise, it is called Buddha. The nature or truth is not to be explained in words. If a false thought be cut off, then the true nature appears, the state of which is called Buddha. Therefore in this doctrine, there is neither division nor rank. At the one thought of his great understanding, one becomes Buddha in the present body as quickly as an image appears in a mirror. From the older times, this doctrine is compared to the Contemplative sect (Zen-shū) founded by Bodhidharma.

The fifth and last doctrine is described as 'completion.' It is called so, because 'one and many are mutually joined, free and without any obstacles.' The fouth doctrine of 'Suddenness' speaks of becoming Buddha at one thought, but it does not yet know the meaning of the non-impediment of every thing of the state of Buddha. In the whole preachings of Buddha, the Ke-gon Sûtra only expounds the doctrine of 'completion.'

There are two kinds in the Ekayâna (Ichi-jō) or the 'one vehicle.' The one is the 'one vehicle of a special doctrine (Betsu-kyō-ichi-jō), that is the Ke-gon Sûtra.

---

9 *Nos.* 175,176,177.

The other is the 'one vehicle of a similar doctrine' (Dō-kyō-ichi-jō), which includes the Saddharma-pu*nd*arîka-sûtra (Ho-ke-kyō) also. So, the name of 'one vehicle' is equally given to the Hokke Sûtra, but that of the 'doctrine of completion' is limited to the Ke-gon Sûtra only.

In short, all the virtues of the state of Buddha are not to be shown, without this doctrine. It says that one destruction is equal to that of all. So, if one cuts off one portion of passions, he is said to cut off all. It also says that one practice is equal to that of all. So, if one practises one practice, he is said to accomplish all. Again, it says that one thought equals immeasurable kalpas. Therefore, one passes over the three Asa*m*khya or countless kalpas within one thought, and becomes Buddha. Thus, in the 'doctrinal division of practice and arrangement' (Gyō-fu-mon), it speaks of the attainment of Buddhahood after passing three different births. But, in the 'division of completion and circulation' (Ennyū-mon), it asserts that when one first raises his thoughts towards the perfect knowledge, he at once becomes fully enlightened. This is the principle of the doctrine of this sect.

CHAPTER VII.

The Ten-dai-shū, or the sect founded on Mount Tendai in China.

I. The doctrine of the sect.

The doctrine of this sect is to encourage all men, whether quick or slow in understanding, to exercise the principle of 'Completion and Suddenness' (Endon), with four doctrinal divisions; one or all of which are taught to men, according to their ability. The object of the doctrine is to make men get an excellent understanding, practise the good discipline, and attain to the great fruit of enlightened. Thus they can become a benefit to their country.

The principle of Completion and Suddenness is the meditation on the middle path. This path is called the inconceivable state. If one understands this principle, all things are in completion. Though beings were originally in the state of completion, they once sank into confusion and began to suffer miseries of existence, without knowing truth. Out of compassion, therefore, Buddha appeared in the world, and preached the truth in several doctrines according fo the circumstances of time and place. There are the four doctrinal divisions of 'Conpletion (En), Secrecy (Mitsu), Meditation (Zen), and Moral Precept (Kai);' which are the means of knowing the principle of Completion.

The following is the regular order of the four doctrinal divisions: 1. The Moral Precept of Completion and Suddenness (En-don-kai), 2. the Action of Meditation (Shi-kwan-gō), 3. the Action of Vairo*k*ana (Sha-na-gō), and 4. the Transmission of the Law of Bodhidharma (Daru-ma-fu-hō).

First, the Moral Precept of Completion and Suddenness is the general character of this sect. So instruction is given on this point as soon as a person enters the sect. Then there is no fixed order as to which of the two Actions should be first undertaken. The Law transmitted from Bodhidharma is again quite a different transmission. It is independent of the order of time, as it is taught to a competent man with a special ceremony.

The Moral Precept of Completion and Suddenness is to receive the perfect and good qualities of Buddha. This is called Ju-kai, or 'receiving the moral precepts,' which are known as the Trividha-sîla (San-ju-jō-kai), or 'threefold pure precepts.'

The first is the Sa*m*bhâra-sîla (Shō-ritsu-gi-kai), or 'Precept of good behaviour,' which prohibits evil. There is no evil that is not destroyed by this precept. When ignorance and passion come to an end by keeping this precept, the state of the Dharma-kâya (Hosshin) or 'spiritual body' of Buddha is attained to. This is called the virtue of destruction (Dantoku).

The second is the Kusala-samgrâha-sîla (Shō-zen-bō-kai), or 'precept of collecting or holding good deeds,' which causes men to practise good workes. There is no good that is not collected in it. This is explained as signifying to raise wisdom, to practise all good works both worldly and religious, neither to take nor to abandon several practices such as the six Pâramitâs or 'perfections,' and to practies good devices (Hō-ben). Then the Sambhoga-kâya (Hō-shin) or 'compensation-body' of Buddha is attained to. This is called the virtue of wisdom (Chi-toku).

The third is the Sattvârtha-kriyâ-sîla (Shō-shu-jō-kai), or 'precept by benevolence towards beings,' which profits beings. There is no being that is not saved by this precept. When all living beings were led to the path of Buddha (or made to follow the doctrine of Buddha), the Nirmâna-kâya (Ō-jin, or Ke-shin) or 'transformed body' is attained to. This is called the virtue of benevolence (On-doku).

These three precepts are the three kinds of the seeds or causes of Buddha. All the Dharmas or 'things' are comprehended in these. Buddha has accomplished all the three, so that he is possessed of perfectly good qualities. These qualities were collected by him for the purpose of giving them to beings.

Therefore it is said in a Sûtra that if beings receive the precepts of Buddha, they at the same time enter the state of Buddhahood. The order of the above three precepts is not fixed. But so far as practice is concerned, the Sambhâra-sîla, or 'precept of good behaviour,' is to be kept first; because it is necessary for all who follow the doctrine of this sect.

Secondly, the Action of Meditation is to practise the excellent contemplation on the middle path, in order to understand the principle of Completion and Suddenness. All the teachings of Buddha in the five periods of his life are comprehended herein. This action belongs to the teaching of completion, so that it is briefly called the Completion (En).

There are also eight divisions of Buddha's doctrine, according to its characteristics suitable to various classes of listners. The 'five periods' (Go-ji) and 'eight divisions of teaching' (Hakkyō) are called the 'doctrine and meditation' (Kyō-kwan) of the Ten-dai sect. The five deriods are called after the titles of the principal Sûtras, namely: 1. The Ke-gon,[1] or Avata*m*saka; 2. the A-gon,[2] or Âgama; 3. the Hō-dō,[3] or Vaipulya; 4. the Han-nya,[4] or Pra*g*ñâ-pâramitâ; and 5. the Hokke,[5] or Saddharma-pu*n*-*d*arîka; and 6. the Ne-han;[6] or Nirvâ*n*a. The eight divisions of teaching are (1) The sudden (Ton), (2)

[1] *Nos.* 87–112. [2] *Nos.* 542–781 etc. [3] *Nos.* 23-86 and many others. [4] *Nos.* 1–22. [5] *Nos.* 133-139. [6] *Nos.* 113–125.

The gradual (Zen), (3) The secret (Hi-mitsu), (4) The indeterminate (Fu-jō), (5) Collection (Zō), (6) Progress (Tsū), (7) Distinction (Betsu), and (8) Completion (En).

Thirdly, the Action of Vairo*k*ana is the doctrine of the highest Yâna or vehicle of the Yoga or union. Those who practise the great doctrine of secrecy of the form and reason, perfect the Siddhi (Shitsu-ji) or 'success,' and benefit the country, are accomplishers of this Law.

This action is the secret performance practised in accordance with the ability of votaries, who wish to understand the perfect way quickly. Therefore it is called the Ji-mitsu or 'secret of matters or forms.' If they understand the meaning of the secrecy of both the form and reason, and reach the state of enlightenment, at the stage of agreement of reason and wisdom, they are quite certain to attain to Buddhahood in the present life.

Fourthly, the Transmission of the Law of Bodhidharma requires only one thought and three rules. Those who begin this practice have to enter at once the spiritual world, and cultivate their mind, wishing to obtain the highest active power of wisdom. Finally, if they were considered to be competent men for the transmission, they are given a sealed diploma in the special ceremony.

II. A history of the sect.

First, the transmission of the Moral Precept of Completion and Suddenness was first received by *S*âkyamuni from Vairo*k*ana (Dai-nichi) Buddha, by whom in turn it was given to the Bodhisattva A*g*ita (A-it-ta, i. e. Maitreya or Mi-roku). Thus it passed through more than twenty Bodhisattvas. Kumâra*g*îva arrived in China on the twentieth day of the twelfth month of the year corresponding to 401 A. D., and transmitted this doctrine to his Chinese disciples. Afterwards E-shi of Nan-gaku and Chi-ki of Ten-dai, whose posthumous title is Chi-sha Dai-shi, greatly revered it, both receiving the secret transmission, called the Tō-chū-sō-jō, or 'transmission within the tower.' The successor of Chi-sha was Kwan-jō of Shō-an. Some generations after, there was the Upâdhyâya (Wa-jō) or 'teacher' Dō-sui of Rō-ya. At his time, Sai-chō (Den-gyō Dai-shi) and Gi-shin (Shu-zen Dai-shi) went to China from Japan. In 805 A. D., they together with twenty others received the transmission of this doctrine from Dō-sui, and returned to Japan.

Sai-chō transmitted it to En-nin (Ji-kaku Dai-shi). This is the origin of the transmission of the Sam-mon or En-ryaku-ji (Hi-ei-zan). Gi-shin transmitted it to En-chin (Chi-shō Dai-shi). This is the origin of the transmission of the Ji-mon or On-jō-ji (Mi-i-dera). After these, it was widely spread over the whole country, and divided into many different schools.

Secondly, the transmission of the Action of Meditation passed through twenty-three patriarchs in India after *S*âkyamuni. In China, E-mon (550 A. D.) followed the views of the Bodhisattva Nâgâr*g*una (Ryū-ju), the thirteenth Indian patriarch, and understood the doctrine of the 'One thought and Three kinds of meditation' (Isshin-San-gwan). He was succeeded by E-shi (Nan-gaku Dai-shi, who died 577 A. D.) and Chi-ki (Ten-dai or Chi-sha Dai-shi, who died 597 A. D.). The latter greatly expounded the doctrine, and it is called ihe transmission of the Spiritual mountain (Ryō-zen, i. e. the G*ri*dhra-kû*t*a (Gi-sha-kutsu) in India, where *S*âkyamuni preached the Saddharma-pu*nd*arîka, the principal Sûtra of this sect). Then it passed through five teachers, from Shō-an Dai-shi to Kei-kei Dai-shi.

In 804 A. D., Den-gyō Dai-shi went to China by Imperial order, and received the transmission of this doctrine from Dō-sui, who was the principal disciple of Kei-kei. After his return to this country, Den-gyō Daì-shi taught it specially to En-chō (Jak-kō Dai-shi) and En-nin (Ji-kaku Dai-shi). This is the transmission of the Sam-mon. In 851 A. D., Chi-shō Dai-shi went to China by Imperial order, and learned the hidden meaning of the doctrine of this sect, under the instruction of Ryō-sho, a successor of Ten-dai Dai-shi in the ninth generation. When he came back to Japan, Chi-shō Dai-shi taught it to Ryō-yū, and completed the system of the doctrine. Since that time, it has been continually handed down. This is the transmission of the Ji-mon.

Thirdly, the Action of Vairo*k*ana, or the great doctrine of the highest vehicle of the secret union, was transmitted in India from the oral intruction of Vairo*k*ana to Va*g*rasattva (Kon-gō-satta), and so on. In China, *S*ubhakarasi*m*ha (Zen-mu i) arrived there from Central India in 716 A. D., and handed the doctrine down to Gi-rin Dai-shi. Soon after, Va*g*ra-bodhi (Kon-gō-chi) also came to China from India; and his disciple Amoghava*g*ra (Fu-kū) went back to India from China and again returned to the latter country. They both transmitted this doctrine to the Chinese Buddhists.

In 805 A. D., Den-gyō Dai-shi met the Â*k*ârya (A-ja-ri) Jun-kyō, a disciple of Gi-rin Dai-shi, and received instruction in this doctrine, and then came home to Japan. In 808, he first practised the secret rite of the Abhisheka (Kwan-jō), or 'sprinkling water on the head,' by Imperial order, in the Takao monastery on Mount Kiyo-taki, on the north-west of Kyōto. Shu-en, Gon-sō, En-chō and some others were then the receivers. This was the day on which this ceremony of Kwan-jō was first performed in Japan.

In 838, Ji-kaku Dai-shi went to China and received instruction in the doctrine of Completion (En), Secrecy (Mitsu), and Meditation (Zen), and also in the

Siddha (Shit-tan) or Sanskrit alphabet, and made clear what had not been known clearly. More especially was he initiated into the secret rites of the great doctrine of Yoga or union. He followed Hō-zen, Gwan-jō and Gi-shin, who were the disciples of the Indian teacher Zen-mu-i's pupil, and received the doctrinal rank of Dai-kyō-ō, or 'great doctrinal king.' In 847, A. D. he came back to this country and became the founder of the Tai-mitsu, i. e. 'secret (Mitsu) doctrine transmitted by the Ten-dai sect.' In some respects, it is far superior to the similar doctrine handed down by the two great teachers (Dai-shi) Den-gyō and Kō-bō. In 854, A. D. it was transmitted to Anne and others. It has since diverged into several schools. This is the transmission of the Sam-mon,

In 853, A. D. Chi-shō Dai-shi went to China, and became the disciple of Hō-zen, and was given two things, viz., a pestle, or a kind of brass mace (Sho or Kine), and a bell (Rei or Suzu), in token of his complete acquirement of the teachings of all the Budhas. He brought back with him several books and other things. Especially was he granted permission by the Emperor to promulgate the 'meditation according to true words' (Shin-gon-shi-kwan). Thus he perfected the meaning of complete secrecy (En-mitsu). Though their genealogical line so far as the Indian and Chinese patriarchs are concerned is the same, Chi-shō Dai-shi was the disciple, in all the three great Laws, of the Âkârya Hō-zen, who praised him greatly and taught him all that was most important. After he came back to Japan, he handed the Laws down to Shū-ei, Kō-sai and others. There is also a school of the transmission of the Siddhi or Sanskrit letters, and some others which belong to the doctrine of Yoga.

Fourthly, the line of the Transmission of the Law of Bodhidharma passed through twenty-eight Indian and seven Chinese patiarchs. In 736, A. D., Dō-sen came to Japan from China and transmitted this Law to Gyō-hyō, who in turn handed it down to Dengyō. In 804, Den-gyō again received instruction in this Law from Shō-nen in China, and taught it to Ji-kaku, who transmitted it to Chō-i, and so on. There are not any different lines in the transmission of this Law among the Sam-mon and Ji-mon.

CHAPTER VIII.

The Shin-gon-shū, or True Word (Mantra) sect.

1. A history of the sect.

The doctrine of this sect is a great secret law. It teaches us that we can attain to the state of the 'Great Enlightened,' that is the state of 'Buddha,' while in the present physical body which was born of our parents (and which consists of six elements, Earth, Water, Fire, Wind, Ether and Knowledge), if we follow the three great secret laws regarding Body, Speech and Thought.

The Tathâgata Mahâvairo*k*ana (Dai-nichi Nyorai) in the state of his Dharma-kâya or 'spiritual body,' preached the doctrine of the secret Mantras or true words (Shin-gon) to his own subjects, in order to show the truth understood by him. This doctrine is recorded in the sûtras such as the Mahâvairo*k*anâbhisambodhi-sûtra (Dai-nichi-kyō,)'[1] and the Va*g*rasekhara-sûtra (Kon-gō-chō-kyō),[2] etc. Although there are numerous words in these sûtras, yet the essential point is nothing but the Ma*nd*ala or the 'circle' of the Two Parts (Ryō-bu) of Va*g*ra-dhâtu (Kon-gō-kai) and Garbha-dhâtu (Tai-zō-kai). The Ma*nd*ala is, therefore, the body or substance of the doctrine of this sect. In the assembly called Ji-shō-e ('self-nature-assembly') in which Buddha preached the law, Va*g*rasattva (Kon-

[1] *No.* 530. [2] *No.* 534.

gō-satta) received the secret Abhisheka (Kwan-jō), i. e. the initiation by sprinkling water upon the head, as the sign of the successor in the Law.

Afterwards the great-minded Nâgârguna (Ryū-myō) saw Vagrasattva in the iron tower in South India, and received the secret doctrine from him, concerning the Two Parts of Vagra and Garbha-dhâtu. Nâgârguna transmitted the Law to his disciple Nâgabodhi (? Ryū-chi), who transmitted it to Vagrabodhi (Kon-gō-chi). Vagrabodhi was a man very learned with regard to many doctrines of Buddhism and other religions, and was expecially well acquainted with the deepest meaning of the doctrine of this sect, which he taught in India for a considerable time.

This is an outline of the transmission of this doctrine in India.

In 720 A. D. Vagrabodhi bringing his disciple Amoghavagra (Fu-kū-kon-gō) arrived in Chō-an, the capital of China. The Emperor Gen-sō of the T'ang or Tō dynasty was then greatly delighted, and ordered him to translate the work called the Yu-ga-nen-ju-hō, or the 'Law of reading and recital in the Yoga doctrine.' He is considered the founder of the secret doctrine of Buddhism in China. After his death, Amoghavagra went back to India, in order to make further researches in his doctrin. In 746 A. D., he came back to China and translated the sacred books, to the number of seventy-seven in all. Kei-kwa of the Sei-ryū-ji was his disciple, who like his master was a very learned man, well versed in the Tripiṭaka and the Two Parts. Thus he propagated this doctrine throughout the Chinese empire.

In 804 A. D., Kū-kai, better known by his posthumous title Kō-bō Dai-shi, went to China from Japan, and became the disciple of Kei-kwa. The latter was very pleased to see him, and said: 'I have waited for yous coming here a long time.' During two months after his arrival there, Kū-kai received secret instruction concerning the Two Parts. In the fourth month, Kei kwa gave him the Abhisheka, or 'sprinkling water on the head' (Kwan-jō), as the sign of successorship, and said: 'The Bhagavat, or the Blessed one, gave the secret key to the truth to Va*g*rasattva, who transmitted it to Nâgâr*g*una, and so on till myself. Now, because I see you are indeed a man well qualified for this learning, I give you the key to the secret great doctrine of the Two Parts. You should propagate it in your native country.' In 806 A. D., he came back to Japan. The Emperor Hei-zei received him cordially, and ordered him to teach it to the people at large.

Thus, from the Tathâgata Mahâvairo*k*ana to Ku-kai, there were eight patriarchs who were the successors in the Law. Besides them there is another series of so-called eight patriarchs who transmitted the Law. Their names are Nâgâr*g*una (Ryū-myō), Nâgabodhi (Ryū-chi), Va*g*rabodhi (Kon-gō-chi), *S*ubhakarasi*m*ha (Zen-mu-i), Amoghava*g*ra (Fu-kū-kon-gō), Kei-kwa, Ichi-gyō and Kū-kai.

Kū-kai had ten great disciples, but two of them were the true successors, namely, Jichi-e and Shin-ga. Gen-nin succeeded them and transmitted the Law to Yaku-shin and Shō-bō. Shō-bō was the founder of the O-no school; and Yaku-shin, of the Hiro-sawa school.

A genealogical table of the succeeding Patriarchs.

India.

1. Mahâvairo*k*ana (Dai-nichi), '*S*âkyamuni's self and inner enlightened body' (Sha-ka-ji-nai-shō-shin).
2. Va*g*rasattva (Kon-gō-satta).
3. Nâgâr*g*una,
4. Nâgabodhi.

China.

5. Va*g*rabodhi.
6. Amoghava*g*ra.
7. Kei-kwa.

Japan.

8. Ku-kai, Kō-bō Dai-shi.
   Jichi-e and Shin-ga.
   Yaku-shin, of the Hiro-sawa school.
   Shō-bō, of the O-no school.

II. The doctrine of the sect.

(a) The doctrinal divisions.

According to this sect, there are two ways of classifying all the doctrines of Buddha. First, as the 'Ten Stages of Thoughts' (Jū-jū-shin), when the doctrines are tabulated and considered consecutively, or lengthwise, of the table. Secondly, as two doctrines, hidden and apparent (Ken-mitsu Ni-kyō), a division which cuts the table across the middle. In the latter divission, all the Laws preached by *S*âkyamun are called apparent doctrine (Ken-gyō); and those delivered by the Dharmakâya (Hosshin), or the spiritual body, hidden or secret doctrine (Mitsu-kyō). The Dharmakâya is the inner enlightened body of Buddha. It is considered by the adharents of the apparent doctrine formless and speechless; but in the hidden doctrine, the Dharmakâya is said to have a form and to preach the Law. The apparent doctrine is that which is adapted to the hearers, like formal conversation with honoured guests. The hidden doctrine, on the other hand, is the Law understood secretly by Buddha and given to his own disciples, like familiar conversation among relatives. This division is, therefore, used to explain the differences of depth and shallowness of the doctrines of this sect and four others, viz., the Hossō, San-ron, Ten-dai and Ke-gon.

The Ten Stages of Thoughts are originally ennumerated in the Chapter on the 'Stages of Thoughts,' in the Dai-nichi-kyō. They are the names used to illustrate ten different stages of the thoughts of living beings. Kū-kai however wisely took them to illustrate the difference of sects. There are also two ways of explaining these thoughts 'crosswise' and 'lengthwise.' 'Crosswise,' they explain the different sorts of objects in the Dharmadhâtu-maṇḍala (Hō-kai-man-da-ra), or the 'circle of the state of things,' and include the meaning of all the doctrines of Buddha. 'Lengthwise,' they explain the gradual improvement of the thoughts of those who practise the doctrine of this sect, from the first moment of their good thought, till the final perfect enlightenment.

The Ten Stages of Thoughts are as follow:—

1. The I-shō-tei-yō-shin, (lit 'different-birth-ram-sheep-thought') is the characteristic of the three evil states of Nârakas or dwellers in hell, Pretas or deperted spirits, and Tiryagyonigata-sattvas or lower animals. The I-shō means ignorant people who are 'different in birth' from the wise men. They are maddened with passions, and can not distinguish good and bad, nor comprehend the reason of cause and effect; but only long for the satisfaction of their appetite and lust, just as a ram. This animal is very low and stupid in nature, and knows nothing but appetite and lust; so that a man who is ignorant of the doctrine of cause and effect is, in India, compared to a ram.

This first Stage of Thought is the gradual cause of pure thought; and when this is once got rid of, the good thought in the second stage is to be substituted.

2. The Gu-dō-ji-sai-shin (lit. 'stupid-boy-holding-fasting-thought') is the characteristic of mankind. The darkness of ignorance of common people is compared with the state of mind of a stupid boy. The fasting is a *Sîla*, or moral precept, to keep the body and speech from disorder. If a man keeps the moral precept, according to the instruction of the teacher and friends, and cultivates his good thought, his state is as the flourishing state of trees and grasses in the spring time. Again, in the case of the practiser of the Shin-gon sect, this is the first state of the Samaya, or meditation, in which he performs the practice of the Three Secrets, regarding Body, Speech and Thought. The five cardinal virtues and the five relationships of Confucianism, and the five precepts of Buddhism are included in this Stage of thought.

3. The Ei-dō-mu-i-shin (lit. 'infant-boy-without-fear-thought') is the characteristic of the heavenly state. The weakness of ignorant people is compared with that of an infant. When they meet good friend, hear the excellent Law, and practise the ten precepts, they will be free from the pains of the three evil states for a time. Hence the name 'mu-i' or 'without

fear.' In the practiser of the Shin-gon sect, it is the state of gradual advance in his practice of the Three Secrets. The opinions of Brahmanism and the ten precepts of Buddhism are included in this Stage of Thought.

4. The Yui-un-mu-ga-shin (lit. 'only-collection-without-self-thought') is the characteristic of the *S*râvakas (Shō-mon), or hearers. There is no self that possesses the supreme power within a living being, which consists of the five Skandhas (Go-un), or collections, namely, Rûpa (Shiki) or form, Vedanâ (Ju) or perception, Sa*m*g*ñ*â (Sō) or name, Sa*m*skâra (Gyō) or conception, and Vi*g*ñâna (Shiki) or knowledge. The Tripi*t*aka of the Hînayâna is altogeher included in this Stage of Thought; and it is the meaning of the doctrine of the Ku-sha sect.

5. The Batsu-gō-in-shu-shin (lit. 'extracting-action-cause-seed-thought') is the characteristic of the Pratyekabuddhas (En-gaku, or Doku-kaku), or 'singly enlightened'. The 'Gō' or action in the term is passion, the 'In' or cause means the twelve causes, and the 'Shu' or seed is the Avidyâ or darkness. From this seed of darkness, passion is raised and an action follows, so that the twelve causes are produced as a link. The Pratyekabuddhas contemplate on these causes and become enlightened, hence the name of 'extracting the seeds or causes of actions.' If these fourth and fifth Stages of Thought are reached,

the practiser of the Shin-gon sect is in the state of meditation, in which any object is contemplated as having no nature, like an image in a mirror, or the reflection of the moon in the water.

6. The Ta-en-dai-jō-shin (lit. 'other-relation-great-vehicle-thought') is the characteristic of the Hossō sect. Having understood the truth that there is nothing but thought, one raises an unlimited compassion, and transfers beings to the other shore of Nirvâna.

7. The Kaku-shin-fu-shō-shin (lit. 'understanding-thought-without-production-thought') is the sharacteristic of the San-ron sect. The Kaku-chin,' or understanding thought,' means to know that the impure thought of passion itself is originally pure. The 'Fu-shō,' or without production,' is the first of eight negative terms to explain the middle path. Taking the first, the other seven are understood. It is said that if the cloud of the false idea of eight confusions is blown away by the wind of the excellent reason explained by eight negations, then the sky of the middle path or truth is clear and calm. If these sixth and seventh stages of Thoughts are reached, the practiser of the Shin-gon sect is in the state of freedom of thought in the meditation of Yoga or union.

8. The Ichi-dō-mu-i-shin (lit.' one-path-without-

doing-thought') is the characteristic of the Ten-dai sect. The 'Ichi-dō,' or 'one path,' is even and equal, and called 'Ichi-nyo,' or 'one suchness' in the Ten-dai sect. The mu-i (Asa*m*sk*r*ita), or 'without doing,' is natural, being called 'Jis-sō or 'true form' in that sect.

9. The Goku-mu-ji-shō-shin (lit. 'extreme-with-out-self-nature-thought') is the characteristic of the Ke-gon sect. The word 'Goku' means extreme or best. In the apparent doctrine (Ken-gyō), the Ke-gon sûtra, or Buddhâvata*m*saka-mahâvaipulya-sûtra, is the best of all; and in that sûtra, the truth is explained in accordance with relation and does not keep the so-called 'self-nature.'

10. The Hi-mitsu-shō-gon-shin (lit. 'secret-hid-dengrave-adornment-thought') is the characteristic of the hidden doctrine. The 'Hi-mitsu,' or 'secret,' is the hidden practice of the Three Secrets of the Tathâgata or Buddha, which adorns the good qualities.

Kū-kai said: 'The apparent doctrine drives away the outer dust, and the Shin-gon, or True Word opens the store (or, shows the inner truth).' Thus the first nine Stages or Thoughts are only the means of stopping passions and driving away the false belief. When he reaches the tenth and last Stage of Thought, the practiser first understands the source and bottom of his own thought, and knows the secret of becoming Buddha by the present body. This is called the true meaning of showing virtue.

1. The Two Parts of the Vagra-dhâtu and Garbhadhâtu.

The *mandala*, or 'circle,' of the Two Parts represents the nature of the reason and wisdom of Buddhas, and also the truth of the from and thought of living beings. The reason why the *mandala* is estabished in this sect is to show that the form and thought of Buddhas and of other living beings, who are not enlightened, equally consist of six elements. In the term Vagra-dhâtu, or Kon-gō-kai (lit. 'diamond element'), the word Vagra has the two senses of hardness and utility. In the former sense it is understood to be compared with the secret truth which is always in existence and not to be broken. In the latter sense, it implies the power of wisdom of the enlightened that destroys the obstacles of passions. The Garbha-dhâtu, or Tai-zō-kai (lit. 'womb element.'), means to take hold of. It is compared with the state of things that are taken hold of within the original body of beings, just as a child is within the body of his mother. These two divisions of the Dhâtus are representations of the nature of form and thought, the one from reason and the other from wisdom, being the principles of this sect. They are, therefore, never to be sought outside of the thought of beings, within which they are really in existence. The important object of the Two Parts of the Vagra and Garbha-dhâtu is to know truly the origin or bottom of one's own thought, and understand the measure or constituents of one's own body.

Although the Two Parts are originally one, yet they are so divided according to the treatment of reason and wisdom. Then the Vagra-dhâtu is the wisdom not separated from reason, and it is that which benefits one's own self. The Garbha-dhâtu is the reason not separated from wisdom, and it is that which benefits others. Again the Garbha-dhâtu consists of the three things of the great meditation, wisdom and compassion, which are Buddba, Vagra and Padma or lotus respectively. These three are technically called Tathâgtânubhâva(Butsu-bu) or Buddha class,' Vagrânubhâva (Kon-gō-bu) or diamond class,' and Padmânubhâva Ren-ge-bu or lotus flower class. The Buddha class corresponds to the Tathâgata Mahâvairokana, (Dai-nichi Nyorai), meaning the perfection of enlightenment. The Vagra class represents the wisdom possessed by Vagra-sattva, which wisdom being firm in nature can destroy all passions even though it has been sunken in the mud of transmigration for a very long time. The Padma class represents the compassion of Avalokitesvara, showing that there is the pure thought within all living beings, which is neither destroyed nor defiled throughout the transmigration in six states of existence, like a lotus flower in mud.

The Va*g*ra-dhâtu explains the five kinds of wisdom (see below), and consists of five classes. These are the Ratnânubhâva (Hō-bu) or 'gem-class' and Karmânubhâva Katsu-ma-bu or 'action class, together with the three classes of the Garbha-dhâtu. The Karma class means to accomplish all the actions, and the Ratna class shows the unlimitedness of virtue and happiness within the perfection of Buddha's enlightenment.

Moreover there is the Ma*nd*ala or circle of nine assemblies in the Va*g*ra-dhâtu, which circle means the perfectness. This Ma*nd*ala is of four kinds, namely, 1. Mahâma*nd*ala, the bodies of all the objects worshipped; 2. Samaya-ma*nd*ala, the sword and other things held by the worthies; 3. Dharma-ma*nd*ala, their Vî*g*a, (Shu-ji) or 'seed' i. e. the mystical letter or syllable forming the essential part of a Mantra, and 4. Karma-ma*nd*ala, their actions.

The Ma*nd*ala of nine assemblies of the Va*g*ra-dhâtu is as follows :—

5 *K*atur-mudrâ-parshad 5	4 Eka-mudrâ-parshad 6	3 Buddhi-gati(?)-parshad 7
6 Pû*g*â-parshad 4	9 Karma-parshad 1	2 Trailokya-vi*g*aya-karma-parshad 8
7 Sûkshma (?)-parshad 3	8 Samaya-parshad 2	1 Trailokya-vi*g*aya-samaya-parshad 9

1. The Karmad-parshad, (Katsuma-e)or 'action assembly' represents the dignified forms and actions of the objects worshipped. This assembly corresponds to the first of the four Ma*nd*alas. If we minutely count them, there are altogether 1061 worshies therin, but generally they are reduced into 37 according to the number of their good qualities, as the 37 Bodhy-aṅgas, or divisions of the perfect knowledge. The 37 worthies of the Karma assembly, the first of the nine assemblies in the Va*g*ra-dhatu, are in the following order:—

West.

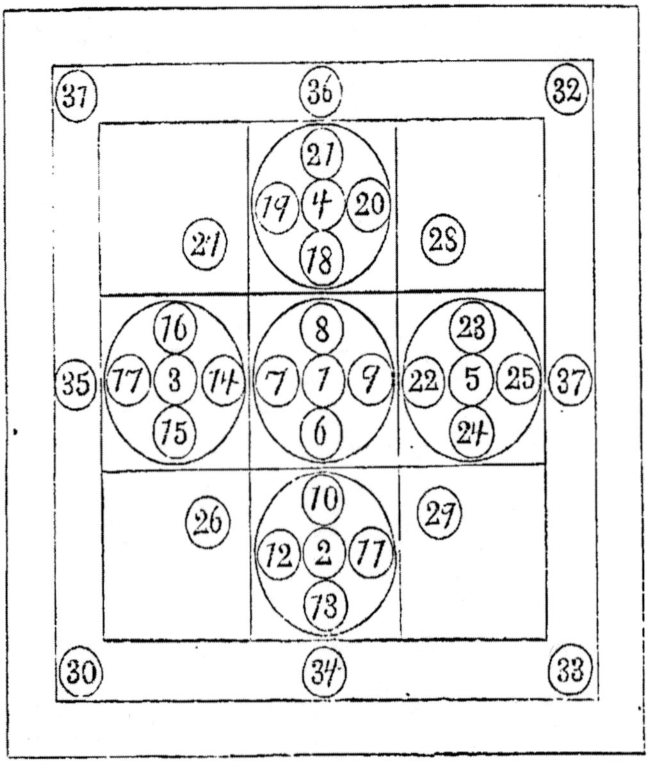

South.

North.

East.

No. 1. Mahâvairo*k*ana, or Dai-nichi ('great sun'), who holds the Mudrâ or seal of the fist of wisdom.

No. 2. Akshobhya, or Ashuku ('immoveable'), who represents the firmness of the thought of Bodhi or perfect wisdom.

No. 3. Ratnasa*m*bhava, or Hō-shō ('gem-birth'), who governs virtues and happiness.

No. 4 Amitâbha, or Amida ('immeasurable light'), who rules over the act of preaching the Law and destroying doubts.

No. 5. Amoghasiddhi, or Fu-kū-jō-ju ('unfailing completion'), i. e. *S*âkyamuni, who rules over the accomplishment of the action of Nirvâ*n*a.

The above five are Buddhas, and the following are Bodhisattvas.

Nos. 6. Sattva-va*g*ra ('being diamond'), 7. Ratna-va*g*ra('gem d.), 8 Dharma-va*g*ra ('law d.'), 9. Karma-va*g*ra ('action d.'); 10. Va*g*ra-sattva ('diamond being'), 11. Va*g*ra-râ*g*a ('d. king'), 12. Va*g*ra-râga ('d. affection'), 13. Va*g*ra-sâdhu ('d. pleasing'); 14. Va*g*ra-ratna ('d. gem'), 15. Va*g*ra-te*g*as ('d. light'). 16. Va*g*ra-ketu ('d. banner'), 17. Va*g*ra-hâsa ('d. laughing'); 18. Va*g*ra, dharma ('d. law'), 19. Va*g*ra-tîksh*n*a ('d. sharp (thing)'), 20. Va*g*ra-hetu ('d. cause'), 21 Va*g*ra-vâ*k* ('d. speech'); 22. Va*g*ra-karma ('d. action), 23. Va*g*ra-raksha ('d. protection'), 24. Va*g*ra-yaksha ('d. tooth (?)'), 25. Va*g*ra-sandhi ('d. firt (?)'); 26. Va*g*ra-lâsa ('d. sport'), 27. Va*g*ra-mâli ('d. garland'), 28. Va*g*ra-gîti ('d. song'), 29. Va*g*ra-n*ri*ti ('d. dancing'); 30. Va*g*ra-dhûpa ('d. incense'), 31. va*g*ra-pushpa ('d. flower'). 32. Va*g*râ-loka (d. light,), 33. Va*g*ra-gandhi ('d. smearing perfume'); 34. Va*g*râṅkusa ('d. hook'), 35. Va*g*ra-bandha (d. tie'), 36.

Vagra-sphota ('d. chain'), and 37. Vagra-ghantâ ('d. bell').

In the above list, Nos. 10–25 are called the sixteen worthies of wisdom, and Nos. 6–9 and 26–37 are those of meditation.

2. The Samaya-parshad, (San-mai-ya-e) or 'agreement assembly' corresponds to the Samaya-mandala. The worthies of this assembly, make the appearance of weapons and Mudrâs or seals, etc., according to their original vow.

3. The Sûkshma (?)-parshad, (Mi-sai-e) or 'minute assembly' corresdonds to the Dharma-mandala. This represents the minute virtues such as five kinds of wisdom of the worthies.

4. The Mahâpûgâ-parshad, (Dai-ku-jō-e) or 'great-worshipping-assembly' corresponds to the Karma-mandala. In this assembly eachof the worthies worships mahâvairokana with gem diadem and wreath, etc.

In each of the above three assemblies (2-4) there are 73 worthies.

5. The Katur-mudrâ-parshad, (Shi-in-e) or four 'seal-assembly' shows the four Mandalas together in this one assembly, in which there are 13 worthies.

In the above five assemblies mahâvairokana (Dai-nichi) is placed in the middle, showing that the cause itself is the effect.

6. The Eka mudra-parshad, (Ichi-in-e) or 'one-seal-assembly' shows the one seal of mahâvairokana and there is only one worthy, viz, mahâvairokana.

7. The Buddhigati (?) -parshad (Ri-shu-e) or 'reason-state-assembly' has 17 worthies, Vagrasattva being placed in the middle. Mahâvairokana of the above six assemblies manifests himself as Vagrasattva in this assembly and benefits living beings. This shows that the effect itself is the cause.

8. The Trailokya-vigaya-karma-parshad (Gō-san-ze-katsu-ma-e) or 'three-world-subduing-action assembly' has 77 worthies. It shows the state of the Mahâ-krodha-kâya ('great-anger-body') manifested by Vagrasattva to destroy the enemies of the three worlds, viz. covetousness, anger and foolishness.

9. The Trailokya-vigaya-samaya-parshad (Gō-san-ze-san-mai-ya-e) or 'three-world-subduing-agreement-assembly' has 73 worthies. It shows the state of the form of Samaya, or agreement of Vagrasattva, who holds the bow and arrow, to warn living beings.

The order of the above nine assemblies is of two kinds. The order given above is from root to completion. If we speak of becoming Buddha, then the Trailokya-vigaya-samaya-parshad is the first, and the Karma-parshad is the end. The former order is from the self-enlightenment to subjugation, and the latter from subjugation to the self-enlightenment.

Thus (437) worthies are counted in the Vagra-dhâtu. But in fact there are innumerable objects worshipped, which are all omitted.

Next the Garbha-dhâtu ('womb element') is called 13 great enclosures (Mahâ-vritis?) The following Mandala, however, omits the shi-dai-go-in ('four-great-protection-enclosure'); so that there are twelve enclosures only:—

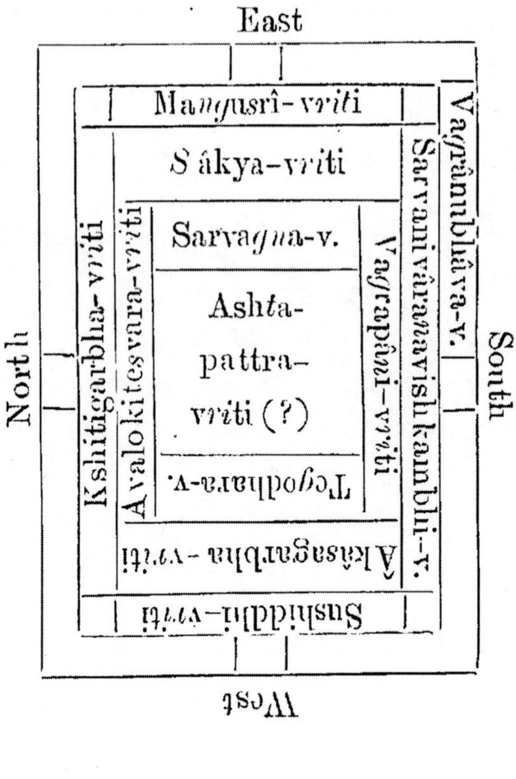

1. The middle Ash*t*a-pattra-v*ri*ti, (Hachi-yōin) or 'eight-leaf-enclosure' is like the following:—

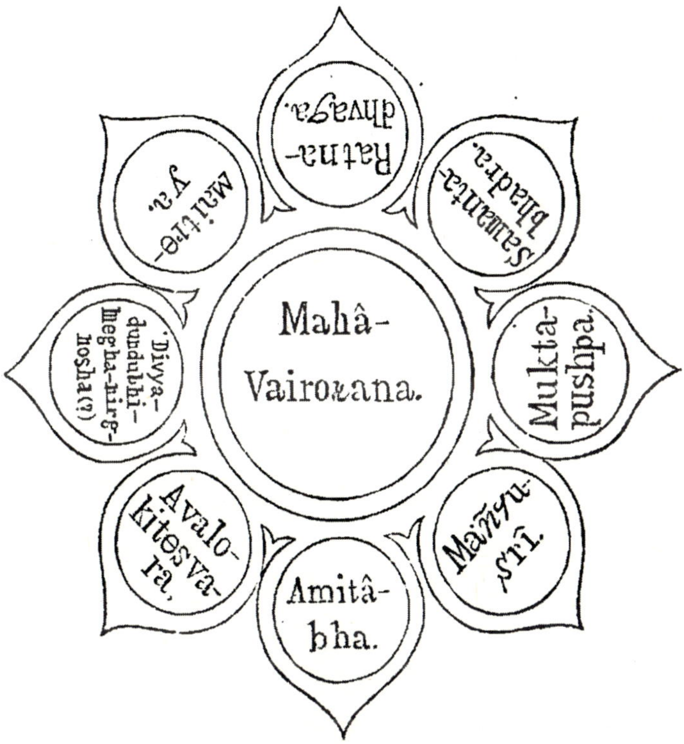

This represents H*ri*daya, or 'heart,' of beings. If they meditate on the lotus flower of their heart, eight petals of the flower are burst open and five Buddhas and four Bodhisattvas appear on them, Mahávairo*k*ana being in the middle. Thus in the middle 'eight-leaf-enclosure,' there are 9 worthies.

2. The Sarva*gñ*a-v*ri*ti (Hen-chi-in) or 'all-knowing-enclosure' on the top contains 7 worthies.

3. The Avalokite*s*vara-v*ri*ti (Kwan-on-in) or 'looking-on-sound-enclosure' on the north contains 37 worthies.

4. The Va*g*rapâ*n*i-v*ri*ti (Kon-gō-shu-in) or 'diamond-hand-enclosure' on the south also contains 37 worthies.

5. The Te*g*odhara-v*ri*ti (Ji-miyō-in) or 'holding-light-enclosure' on the bottom contains 5 worthies.

6. The *S*âkya-v*ri*ti (Sha-ka-in) or 'able-one-enclosure' on the top contains 39 worthies.

7. The Man*g*u*s*rî-v*ri*ti (Mon-ju-in) or 'lucky-enclosure' on the top contains 35 worthies.

8. The Sarvanivâra*n*avishkambhi-v*ri*ti (Jo-gai-shō-in or 'removing-covering-obstacle-enclosure' on the south contains 9 worthies.

9. Ths Kshitigarbha-v*ri*ti (Ji-zō-in) or 'earth-womb-enclosure' on the north contains 9 worthies.

10. The Âkâ*s*agarbha-v*ri*ti (Ko-ku-zō-in) or 'sky-womb-enclosure' on the bottom contains 28 worthies.

11. The Susiddhi-v*ri*ti (So-shitsu-ji-in) or 'well-perfection-enclosure' on the bottom contains 8 worthies.

12. The outside Va*g*rânubhâva-v*ri*ti (Kon-gō-bu-in) or 'diamond-class-enclosure' on the four sides contains altogether 205 worthies.

The total number of the worthies in the above twelve enclosures is 428. Again there are altogether 865 worthies in the Two Parts; but in reality there are endless objects worshipped in the state of things throughout the ten directions, which are all included in these Two Parts. Even if we should know that one Buddha exists within our own body, our merit would be immeasurable. How much more there exist originally unlimited worthies within the heart of all living beings equally. This is truly the extreme secret.

(c) The unimpeded state of six elements

The shan-mahâbhûtas (Roku-dai) or 'six great elements' are earth, water, fire, air, ether, and knowledge. These six exist everywhere, so that they are called Mahâbhûtas, or great elements. If they are divided among the Two Parts, the first five are reason, corresponding to the Garbha-dhâtu, or Tai-zō-kai; and the last is wisdom, being the Vagra-dhâtu, or Kon-gō-kai. However, the reason and wisdom are originally not two; so that there is no knowledge besides the first five elements, and vice versâ. So, if the sixth element vigñâna, or knowledge, is divided into five elements, these are as many kinds of wisdom, technically called Go-chi, or 'five-wisdom.' They are as follow: — 1. The Dharma-dhâtu-prakrit-gñâna, or Hō-kai-tai-shō-chi ('thing-element-substance-nature-wisdom'), corresponds to the element ether, being the wisdom to become the substance of things. 2. The Âdarsana-*gñâna*, or Dai-en-kyō-chi ('great-round-mirror-wisdom'), corresponds to the element earth, manifesting the images of all things just as in the mirror. 3. The Samatâ-*gñâna*, or Byō-dō-shō-chi ('even-equal-nature-wisdom') corresponds to the element fire, making no distinction between this and that, while looking at the things. 4. The Praty-avekshana-*gñâna*, or Myō-kwan-zatsu-chi ('well-looking-considering-wisdom') corresponds to the element water, being the wisdom that governs the act of preaching the Law and destroying doubts, and that distinguishes clearly what is right or wrong. 5. The K*ri*tyânush*th*âna-*gñâna*, or Jō-sho-sa-chi ('wisdom of accomplishing what is to be done') corresponds to the element air, being the wisdom of completing the good action of helping both one's own self and others. This comparison is however not permanent.

The unimpeded state of these elements one with another is compared with the rays of light of many different lamps. The six elements of Buddha are not hindered by those of unenlightened beings. Therfore there is no being besides Buddha, and no Buddha besides being. Such is the unimpeded state of the six elements.

(d) The Yoga or union of the three secrets (San-mitsu-sō-ō).

The three secrets are the three actions of body, speech and thought. These are originally even and equal. Body is equal to speech, and speech is equal to thought. They all exist everywhere in the Dharma-dhâtu, or element of things, and are called the three secrets even and equal to all Buddhas. Speaking briefly of the form of the Dharma-dhâtu, the apparent form of all things is that of the five elements; and it is the secret of body. This form or body produces sound, and it is the secret of speech. This form has the power (Kō-nō) and it is the secret of thought. These three secrets exist in things both animate and inanimate. Therefore if the wind blows trees, waves beat rocks, and a man raises hands, moves feet, speaks and keeps silence, all are in the three secrets. But these are the states understood by Buddha only, and not approached by an ordinary man; so that they are called secrets. Buddha taught us the rules of Mudrâs or seals and Mantras or True Words, etc., in order to cause ignorant people unite with the state of Buddha. This is the meaning of union (Yoga). It makes no difference between the 'equal' three secrets of Buddha and the 'distinct' three secrets of beings. The three secrets are originally equal without distinction, but ignorant people make distinction of them falsely. Therefore Buddha adds his three secrets to those of beings. This addition is however not that of two different things. The nature of the secrets of beings are originally not different from those of Buddha's. But ignorant people do not know it. So Buddha teaches them to understand and meditate on this. Such meditation and understanding are those of Buddha, so that there is the meaning of adding the three secrets of Buddha to the three actions of beings. If our practice is ripe in imitating the action of Buddha and becomes equal to the three secrets of Buddha, then there is the meaning of union (Yoga). It is said: San-mitsu-sō-ō-soku-shin-jō, or 'Three secrets united, the present body becomes (Buddha).'

(e) The attainment to the state of Buddha by the present body (Soku-shin-jō-butsu).

There are three kinds of explaining this subject, viz, Ri-gu ('reason-completed'), Ka-ji ('adding-holding'), and Ken-toku ('apparent-obtaining'). The first is explained in the following word: The true form of body and thought of all living beings is the Ma*nd*ala, or circle, of the Two Parts of Va*g*ra and Garbha-dhâtu. The flesh body is the reason of the first five elements, and it is the Garbha-dhâtu; while the thought is the wisdom of the sixth element, knowledge, and it is the Va*g*ra-dhâtu. These wisdom and reason are originally completed in all living beings. This is technically called Ri-gu-soku-shin-jō-butsu, or 'the attainment of Buddhahood by the present body completed in reason.'

The second is to make the originally completed Ma*nd*ala or circle opened and manisfested by the power of 'adding and holding' (Ka-ji) of the three secrets.

The third is to reach the origin of one's own thought, obtain the Ma*nd*ala, and attain to the final state of perfect enlightenment, after completing the practice of the three secrets.

These three kinds of becoming Buddha are only difference in explanation, and in reality they are one and no distinction.

The virtue completed in one's self and not obtained from others is the character of the first (Ri-gu). The ignorant people do not know it, but can perceive it by the power of 'adding and holding' of the Three Secrets. This is the second (Ka-ji). The third is to complete the practice and become the perfectly enlightened (Ken-toku).

The above sketch is only an outline of the doctrine of this sect. If one wants to examine it more minutely, he has to read the three principal Sûtras, Dai-nichi-kyō,[4] So-shitsu-ji-kyō,[5] and Kon-gō-chō-kyō,[6] and also many works called Gi-ki, or 'ceremonial rules.' Besides them, there are several works written by Kū-kai, Kō-bō Dai-shi, who established this Shin-gon sect in Japan.

---

[4] *No.* 530. [5] *No.* 533. [6] *No.* 534.

CHAPTER IX.

The Jō-do-shū, or Pure Land sect.

1. A history of the sect.

Buddhism was first introduced into China from India, in 67 A. D. In 252 A. D., an indian scholar of the Tripiṭaka, Saṃghavarman (Kō Sō-gai) by name, came to China and translated the great Amitâyus-sûtra (Mu-ryō-ju-kyō)[1] or Larger Sukhâvatî-vyûha in two volumes. This is the first and longest of the three sacred books of this sect. This Sûtra gives a history of the Tathâgata Amstâbha from the first spiritual impulses which led him to the attainment of Buddhahood in remote Kalpas down to the present time when he dwells in the western world called Sukhâvatî (Goku-raku, or 'happy'), where he receives all living beings from every direction, helping them to turn away from confusion and to become enlightened.

In 400 A. D., Kumâragîva (Ra-jū) came to China from the kingdom of Kharachar (Ki-ji) and produced a translation of the small Amitâyus-sûtra (A-mi-da-kyō)[2] or Smaller Sukhâvatîvyûha in one volume. This is the shortest of the three sacred books. It is taught in this Sûtra that if man keeps in his memory the name of Buddha Amitâbha one day or seven days, the Buddha together with Bodhisattvas will come

[1] *No.* 27. [2] *No.* 200.

and meet him at the moment of his death in order to let him be born in the Pure Land Sukhâvatî; and that this matter has equally been approved by all other Buddhas of ten different directions.

In 424 A. D., Kâlayasas (Kyō-ryō-ya-sha) arrived in China from India and translated the Amitâyus-dhyâna-sûtra (Kwan-mu-ryō-ju-kyō)[3] in one volume. This is the second longest of the three sacred books. An outline of this sûtra is as follows: Vaidehî, consort of king Bimbisâra of Magadha, seeing the wicked actions of her son A*g*âtasatru, began to feel weary of this world Sahâ (Sha-ba, or 'enduring'). *S*âkyamuni then taught her how to be born in the Pure Land Sukhâvatî instructing her in the method of being born in that world, enumerating three kinds of good actions. The first is worldly goodness, which includes good actions in general, such as filial piety, respect for elders, loyalty, faithfulness, etc. The second is the goodness of *S*îla or morality, in which there are differences between the priesthood and the laity. In short, however, all that do not oppose the general rule of reproving wickedness and exhorting to the practice of virtue are included in this goodness. The third is the goodness of practice, which includes that of the four Satyas or truths and the six Pâramitâs or perfections. Besides these all other pure and good actions such as the reading and recital of the Mahâ-

[3] *No.* 198.

yâna-sûtras, persuading others to hear the Law, and thirteen kinds of goodness to be practised by fixed thought are comprised in this. Towards the end of the Sûtra Buddha says: 'Let not one's voice cease, but ten times complete the thought, and repeat Namo'mitâbhâya Buddhâya (Na-mu-a-mi-da-butsu), or adoration to Amitâbha Buddha.' This practice is the most excellent of all.

Buddha teaches us in his doctrine the truth of cause and effect from his right wisdom and understanding. Bad seed produces bad fruit, and good seed produces good fruit, just as red pepper is pungent and sugar-cane sweet according to their own seeds. This is quite natural. No one doubts about it. Therefore the Sûtra is quite true when it says that the right cause of the three kinds of goodness gains the right fruit of nine different stages in the Pure Land Sukhâvatî.

Depending on the three Sûtras above mentioned, there were three patriarchs in India, who preached the doctrine of the Pure Land. They were Asvaghosha (Me-myō), Nâgârguna (Ryū-ju) and Vasubandhu (Se-shin), who were born in India six, seven and nine hundred years after Buddha respectively.

In China, E-on (died 416 A. D.) of the Shin dynasty, Don-ran (d. 542) of the Gi dynasty, and Dōshaku and Zen-dō (both lived about 600-650) of the Tō (T'ang) dynasty chiefly taught this doctrine.

Especially Zen-dō used his whole power for the Kwan-mu-ryō-ju-kyō, and wrote a new commentary on it in four volumes. He understood thoroughly the thought of Buddha, and clearly explained the text. In this way, he really excelled his predecessors, such as Jō-yō, Ten-dai, Ka-jō and others. He said himself that he had laid a rule for all ages. This is not at all an exaggsration.

Afterwards Hosshō went to Mount Go-dai, where he worshipped *Mañgusrî*, and wrote a number of verses, collectively called Go-e-san, or 'verses for five assemblies.' Another teacher named Shō-kō is said to have seen light coming out from the books left by Zen-dō in the temple of Haku-ba-ji, or 'white horse temple.' All these were the benefits left by Zen-dō after his death. During his life-time, the influence of his teaching was so great that the most people abstained from fish or flesh and the market meat of the capital was not sold much. This is the reason why he is generally considered as the greatest master of this doctrine in China.

About five centuries after Zen-dō, in 1133 A. D., a boy was born in the Uruma family of the province of Mimasaka in Japan. This boy's name was Sei-shi-maru. In his ninth year, he was converted by his father's dying words, and when he was fourteen years old, he went up to mount Hi-ei where in the following year, he shaved his head and received the precepts. Then his name was changed to Gen-ku. In his eighteenth year he retired to kurodani, and five times read through the five thousand volumes of the Tripiṭaka. He did this for the purpose of finding out the way for the ordinary and ignorant people of the present day to escape from misery. Taking this opportunity he studied Zen-do's commentary already alluded to. He repeated his examination altogether eight times. At last he noticed a passage in it, beginning with the words 'Chiefly remember or repeat the name of Amitâbha with a whole and undivided heart' (Is-shin-sen-nen-mi-da-myō-gō), etc. Then he at once understood the thought of Zen-dō, who taught in his work that whoever at any time practises to remember Buddha or calls his name only once, will gain the right effect of going to be born in the Pure Land after death. Gen-kū then abandoned all sorts of practices, which he had hitherto followed for years; and began to repeat the name of Buddha Amitâbha sixty thousand times a day. This event occurred in 1175 A.D., when Gen-kū was in his forty-third year. The name of Jō-do-shū or Pure Land sect was first known in Japan in this year. This account is given in the Choku-shu-den, or Life of Gen-kū compiled by Imperial Order, and the Sen-jaku-shū, that is Gen-kū's own work.

Gen-kū was very famous in his life-time. He

became the spiritual preceptor of the three Emperors Taka-kura, Go Shira-kawa, and Go To-ba. After his death, his biography was compiled in forty-eight volumes, by Imperial Order. It was copied by three other Emperors Fushi-mi, Go Fushi-mi, and Go Ni-jō.

Before Gen-kū, there were eminent priests in Japan, such as Kū-ya, Ei-kwan, and E-shin also called Gen-shin, who all preached this doctrine, but had no successors. Gen-ku had hundreds of disciples. Among them, Shō-kō of Chin-zei and Zenne of Sei-zan were the principal ones. At present there are myriads of monasteries and priests of this sect in the Empire.

II. The doctrine of the sect.

Dō-shaku says in his work, the An-raku-shū, that there are two divisions in the teaching of *S*âkya-muni, namely, Mahâyâna (Dai-jō) and Hînayâna (Shō-jō). In the former again, there are two gates, viz., the Holy Path (Shō-dō) and the Pure Land (Jō-do). The Hînayâna is the doctrine by which the immediate disciples of Buddha, and those of the period of five hundred years after Buddha, practised the three *S*ikshâs (San-gaku) or trainings of Adhisîla (Kai) or 'higher morality,' Adhi*k*itta (Jō) or 'higher thought,' and Adhipra*gñ*â (E) or 'higher learning,' and obtained in their present life the four holy fruits of Srota-âpanna, Sak*ri*d-âgâmin, Anâgâmin, and

Arhat. The gate of the Mahâyâna is also the doctrine by which man practises the three trainings above mentioned; and in his present life, he understands the three virtues of Dharma-kâya (Hosshin) or 'spiritual body,' Pra*gñ*â (Han-nya) or 'wisdom,' and Moksha (Ge-datsu) or 'deliverance.' The man who is able to do this is no ordinary one, but has natural vigour, and is supposed to possess merit produced from good actions performed in a former state of existence. The firmness of this man's heart is as hard as a rock, and his fearlessness of any obstacles is like a brave soldier's crushing his enemy. The doctrine which causes man to do so, is called the gate of the Holy Path, and the man is called one who enters the holy state in this world. During fifteen hundred years after Buddha, there were such personages in the world from time to time. The flourishing state of Buddhism at that period and the lives of those eminent priests are to be seen from several compilations of their memoirs.

Now, as the present time belongs to the Latter Day of the Law (Mappō), people become insincere, their covetousness and anger daily increase, and their contentions yearly arise. The three trainings already alluded to are the correct causes of deliverance; but if people think them as useless as last year's almanac, when can they complete their deliverance? Gen-kū, therefore, deeply thinking of this, shut up the gate of the Holy Path and opened that of the Pure Land. For in the former the effect of deliverance is expected in this world by the three trainings of morality, thought and learning; and in the latter the great fruit of going to be born in the Pure Land after death is expected through the sole practice of repeating Buddha's name. Moreover it is not easy to accomplish the cause and effect of the Holy Path. But those of the doctrine of the Pure Land are both very easy to be completed. This difference is compared with going by land and water in Ryū-ju's work. Both the gates of the Holy Path and Pure Land, being the docrine of Mahâyâna, have the same object to attain to the state of Buddhahood. As the time and people for the two gates are not the same, the dotrines are necessarily different, just as one uses a carriage on the land, while another employs a ship upon the water.

The doctrines preached by *S*âkyamuni are altogether eighty-four-thousand in number; that is to say, he taught one kind of people one doctrine such as the Holy Path, and another, as that of the Pure Land. The doctrine of the Pure Land was not only shown by Gen-kū, but also by Zen-dō in his great work. Again this was not only pointed out by Zen-dō, but it was derived from the Sûtra preached by the great teacher *S*âkyamuni. It is said that when Zen-dō was writing his commentary, he prayed for a wonderful exhibition of supernatural power. Then there appeared to him in a dream every night a dignified priest, who gave him instruction on the division of the text in his first volume. Therefore the author (Zen-dō) treats his own work, as if it were the work of Buddha; and says that no one is allowed either to add or take away even a word or sentence of the book. This is the reason why Gen-kū quotes the three Sûtras and Zen-dō's commentary as the texts in his own work, the Sen-jaku-shū.

If one wants to know the doctrine of the Pure Land, he must believe in the words of Buddha. Śâkyamuni was the sage who perceived the three times, past, present and future, which are just as yesterday, to-day and to-morrow. Among the Indian heretics, there were some who spoke of the future, but their account of it was not accurate; and there was none who spoke of the past. Now the modern people speak of the present life only, and do not know the past and future. Buddha alone knows the three without any mistakes.

The Pure Land is the western world where Buddha Amitâbha lives. It is perfectly pure and free from faults. Therefore it is called the Pure Land. Those who wish to go there, will certainly be born there; but otherwise they will not. This world Sahâ (Shaba), on the contrary, is the effect of the actions of all beings, so that even those who do not wish to be born here, are also obliged to come. This world is called the path of pain, because it is full of all sorts of pains, such as birth, old age, disease, death, etc. This is therefore a world not to be attached to, but to be disgusted with and separated from. One who is disgusted with this world Sahâ and who is filled with desire for that world Sukhâvatî will after death be forn there. Not to doubt about these words of Buddha even in the slightest degree is called the deep faith; but if one entertains any doubts, he will not be born there. For this reason, Ryū-ju said: 'In the great sea of the Law of Buddha, faith is the only means to enter.' This is an outline of the doctrine of this sect.

CHAPTER X.

The Zen-shū or Contemplative sect.

I. A doctrine of the sect.

The word Zen is a shortened form of the term Zen-na, which is a transliteration of the Sanskrit word Dhyâna, or contemplation.

The general character of the doctrine of this sect is briefly explained by the eight Chinese words, Kyō-ge-betsu-den-fu-ryū-mon-ji, or Special transmission independent of a common teaching and not established on any letter or word. Besides all the doctrines of the Mahâyâna and Hînayâna, whether hidden or apparent, there is, therefore, one distinct line of transmission of a secret doctrine, which is not subject to any utterance at all. According to this doctrine, one is directly to see the so-called key to the thought of Buddha or the nature of Buddha, by his own thought, being free from the multitude of different doctrines, the number of which is said to reach eighty-four thousand. In short, it is the truth made apparent by one's own thought.

II. A history of the sect.

(a) The transmission of the doctrine.

When the Bhagavat (Se-son, or 'Blessed') *S*âkyamuni was at the assembly on Mount G*ri*dhrakû*t*a (Ryō-zen) or 'vulture's peak,' there came the heavenly king Mahâbrahman (Dai-bon), who offered Buddha a flower of a golden colour, and asked him to preach the Law. The Blessed one only took the flower and held it in his hand, but said no word. No one in the whole assembly could understand what he meant. The venerable Mahâkâsyapa alone smiled. Then the Blessed one said to him: 'I have the wonderful thought of Nirvâ*n*a (Ne-han), the eye of the right law, which I shall now give to you.' (See tho Dai-bon-tennō-mon-butsu-ketsu-gi-kyō, or 'Sûtra on the Great Bramnan king's questioning Buddha to dispel a doubt.') This is called the doctrine of thought transmitted by thought.

Kâ*s*yapa gave it to Ânanda, who gave it in turn to *S*a*n*avâsa, and so on till Bodhidharma, the twenty-eighth patriarch. The following is a list of the names of these patriarchs:—

1. Mahâkâ*s*yapa (Ma-ka-ka-shō).
2. Ânanda (A-nân-da).
3. *S*a*n*avâsa (Shō-na-wa-shu)
4. Upagupta (U-ba-kiku-ta)
5. Dh*ri*taka (Dai-ta-ka).
6. Mi*kkh*aka (Mi-sha-ka).
7. Vasumitra (Ba-shu-mtisu).
8. Buddhanandi (Butsu-da-nan-dai).
9. Buddhamitra (Fu-da-mi-ta).
10. Pâr*s*va (Ha-ri-shu-ba).
11. Pu*n*yaya*s*as (Fu-na-ya-sha).
12. A*s*vaghosha (A-na-bo-tei).

13. Kapimala (Ka-bi-mo-ra).
14. Nâgârguna (Na-gya-a-ra-ju-na).
15. Kânadeva (Ka-na-dai-ba).
16. Râhulata (Ra-go-ra-ta).
17. Samghanandi (Sō-gya-nan-dai).
18. Samghayasas (Ka-ya-sha-ta).
19. Kumârata (Ku-mo-rà-ta).
20. Gayata (Sha-ya-ta).
21. Vasubandhu (Ba-shu-han-dzu).
22. Manura (Ma-do-ra).
23. Haklenayasas (Kaku-roku-na).
24. Simha (Shi-shi).
25. Vasasuta (Ba-sha-shi-ta).
26. Punyamitra (Fu-nyo-mit-ta).
27. Pragñâtara (Han nya-ta-ra).
28. Bodhidharma (Bo-dai-daru-ma).

Bodhidharma was the third son of a king of the Kâshis, in South India. Thinking that the time of teaching his doctrine of contemplation in the East had come, he arrived in China, in the first year of the Fu-tsū period under the Ryō dynasty, 520 A. D. Bodhidharma then taught the Emperor Bu the secret key of Buddha's thought, who was, however, not yet able to understand it. So leaving there, he crossed the river Yō-shi, and entered the dominion of the Northern Gi. In the Shō-rin-ji (the name of a monastery) on Mount Sū he sat down cross-legged in meditation, with his face to a wall, for nine years. During that period, people did not know him, and called him simply the Wall-gazing Brâhma*n*a.

Afterwards he had a number of disciples, but they had different views, that are called the transmission of either skin, flesh, or bone of the teacher. Only one of them, E-ka by name, got the whole body of his teaching. The fifth patriarch from Bodhidharma was Kō-nin. Among his disciples, there were two worthy men, E-nō and Jin-shū. The latter taught the doctrine to his followers in the northern part of China, and established the Northern sect. E-nō did so in the southern part, founding the Southern sect.

The Southern sect was soon divided into five schools known as Rin-zai, Gi-gō, Sō-tō, Un-mon and Hō-gen. In the first school Rin-zai, there were two subdivisions, namely, Yō-gi and O-ryū. All these are collectively called the five houses and seven schools of the Southern sect. There was no division of the Northern sect.

As to the propagation of this doctrine in Japan, Dō-sen, a disciple of one of Jin-shū's pupils, came over from China to this country, in 729 A. D. He lived in the Dai-an-ji, and handed down the doctrine of the Northern Contemplation to Gyō-hyō, who transmitted it to Sai-chō, the establisher of the Tendai sect in Japan.

The Southern branch of the Contemplative sect was first transferred to Japan by Ei-sai, of the Ken-nin-ji. He went to China in 1168 A. D., and became the disciple of Kyo-an, of the Man-nen-ji. By him the Rin-zai sect was first established in the Empire. After that, the successors of the Rin-zai school became numerous. Shō-ichi of the Tō-fuku-ji and But-kō of the En-gaku-ji were both the disciples of Yō-gi's ninth generation. Shō-ichi had a disciple named Dai myō, who had the Nan-zen-ji built. Mu-sō of the Ten-ryū-ji was taught by a pupil of But-kō. Dai-kaku of the Ken-chō-ji was a disciple in the tenth generation of Yō-gi, and Dai-tō of the Dai-toku-ji, the eleventh. The latter had an active disciple named Kwan-zan, who founded the Myō-shin-ji.

Thus the Ken-nin-ji, Tō-fuku-ji, En-gaku-ji, Nan-zen-ji, Ten-ryū-ji, Ken-chō-ji, Dai-toku-ji, Myō-shin-ji, together with the Sō-koku-ji, are called the nine principal monasteries of the Rin-zai sect.

The Sō tō sect was established here by Dō gen of the Ei-hei-ji, who went to China in 1223 A. D., and became a disciple of Nyo-jō of Ten-dō. When he returned to Japan, the Emperor Go-Sa-ga paid great respect to him, gave him a purple robe as a gift, and addressed him by the title of Buppō Zen-ji, or the Teacher of Contemplation in the Law of Buddha.

Shō-kin of the Sō-ji-ji was a disciple in the fourth generation of Dō-gen. The Emperor Go Dai-go gave him a purple robe, and called his monastery as the principal one of the sect. The Emperor Go Mura-kami gave him the posthumous title of Butsu-ji Zen-ji.

The Ei-hei-ji and Sō-ji-ji are called the two principal monasteries of the Sō-tō sect in Japan.

Afterwards, in the reign of the Emperor Go Kō-myō, 1644-1654 A. D., a Chinese priest named In-gen came to Japan. He was a disciple by descent of the Ō-ryū school, a branch of the Rin-Zai, and established here the Ō-baku sect.

The Rin-Zai, Sō-tō and O-baku are called the three Japanese Contemplative sects or schcools.

(b) The origin of the Southern and Northern sects.

As it has been mentioned, there have long existed two branches of the Contemplative sect in China as the southern and Northern sects. This divission took place between the two worthies, E-nō and Jin-shū, disciples of Kō-nin, the fifth patriarch, On a certain occassion, the teacher told all his disciples that the right law of Buddha was difficult to understand, and that they should not merely rely upon the words of their master, but their own views. So theywere ordered to compose verses expressing their own opinions, with the condition that he whose verses were correct in meaning should he given the cloaks and the alms-bowl of *S*âkyamuni, transmitted through the Indian and Chinese patriarchs, as the symbols of the rightful successor. Then the venerable Jin-shū, the head of seven hundred disciples, composed the following verses:—

"The body is like the knowledge tree.
The mind is like a mirror on its stand.
It should be constantly and carefully brushed,
Lest dust should be attracted to it."[1]

His teacher recognized it and said: 'If men in future should practise their religion according to this view, they would have an excellent reward.' This is the origin of the Northern sect.

The venerable E-nō was then only a servant, employed to clean rice in a mortar, the pestle of which was worked by the foot. Hearing of Jin-shū's verses secretly, he remarked that it was very beautiful, but not perfectly good. So saying, he wrote verses as follow:—

"There is no such thing as a knowledge tree.
There is no such thing as a mirror stand.
There is nothing that has a real existence.
Then how can dust be attracted?"[1]

On seeing these verses, the teacher Kō-nin at once gave him the symbols of the cloaks and bowl. This is the origin of the Southern sect. The doctrine of this sect is a most sublime one of thought transmitted

[1] Dr. Edkins, Chinese Buddhism, p. 162.

by thought, being entirely independent of any letters or words. It is in later period called the Patriarch's Contemplation (So-shi-zen), because it contains the key of the thought of the Indian patriarch Bodhidharma. But it is a mistake that some call the doctrine of the Northern sect the Tathâgata's Contemplation (Nyo-rai-zen).

Thus in China there have been the two divisions of the Southern and Northern sects and the former was subdivided into five houses and seven schools as before said. Three schools of the Southern sect exist in Japan at present. But all these are the descendants of Bodhidharma, and the principle of their doctrine is only to show what appears in one's own thought. If one wishes to understand the true meaning of the doctrine, he must study it under the instruction of a right teacher. There are however numerous works containing the instructive words of the teachers of different schools. They are called Goroku, or 'Records of sayings,' which may be serviceable in understanding the doctrine of this sect.

CHAPTER XI.

The Shin-shū, or True sect.

1. A history of the sect.

The full name of the sect is Jō-do-shin-shū, or 'True sect of the Pure Land.' The Pure Land is the term antithetical to that of the Shō-dō or Holy Path. The object of the followers of this sect is to be born in the Pure Land Sukhâvatî of Amitâbha. The third word Shin or 'True' is used to show the antithesis to the Gon-ke-hō-ben, or 'Temporary expedients.' Among those who follow the doctrine of the Pure Land, there are several different systems of teaching, which are as follow:— Some say that we should practise various good works, bring our stock of merits to maturity, and be born in the Pure Land. Others say that we should repeat only the name of Amitâbha Buddha, in order to be born in his Pure Land, by the merit produced from such repetition. These doctrines are all considered as yet the temporary expedients. To rely upon the power of the Original Prayer of Amitâbha Buddha with the whole heart and give up all idea of Ji-riki or 'self power' is called the truth. This truth is the doctrine of this sect. Therefore it is called the Shin-shū, or True sect.

Shin-ran, the founder of the sect, makes in his work a clear distinction of four systems with as many terms known as the 'two pairs' and 'four folds' or tiers (Ni-sō Shi-jū). They are: 1. The 'lengthwise going-out' (Shu shutsu), that is the attainment of Enlightenment after long practice and perseverance, through many kalpas or periods, in the way of holy men. 2. The 'lengthwise passing-over' (Shu-chō), which refers to Enlightenment in this life, or to the attainment of Buddhahood in the present existence. 3. The 'crosswise going-out' (Ō-shutsu), i. e. the attainment of birth in a region where the state of beings is like that of those in the womb, and a border-land, or species of limbo, adjoining the Pure Land. The imperfection of this birth is the result of carelessness and doubt. 4. The 'crosswise passing-over' (Ō-chō), i. e. birth in the true Land of Amitâbha Buddha according to his Original Prayer.[1] Of these four systems, the fourth is the doctrine of the Shin-shū.

There are three principal sacred books of this sect, all of which contain *S*âkyamuni's teaching on the doctrine of going to be born in Sukhâvatî. These are the same Sûtras as those mentioned in the previous chapter on the Jō-do-shū. The Dai-mu-ryō-ju-kyō,[2] or Larger Sukhâvatîvyûha, the longest of the three Sûtras, is taken as a special text book. This is because in it are spoken the forty-eight Original

[1] See note 6 in Mr. James Troup's translation of the Shin-shū-kyō-shi. [2] *No.* 27.

Prayers of Amitâbha, the eighteenth of which is the foundation of the doctrine of the 'crosswise passing-over' (Ō-chō).

This doctrine was transmitted at various times and in different places by the so-called 'Seven High Priests' (Shichi-kō-sō), who were the patriarchs of the three countries of India, China and Japan. They were the two Bodhisattvas Nâgâr*g*una (Ryū-ju) and Vasubandhu (Ten-jin) of India, Don-ran, Dō-shaku and Zen-dō of China, and Gen-shin and Gen-kū of Japan. Their works are most minute in explaining the doctrine of the sect, for which reason the authors are reckoned as patriarchs. The seventh patriarch Gen-kū also called Hō-nen was the teacher of Shin-ran, the founder of the sect.

Shin-ran was a scion of the Fuji-wara family (born 1173 and died 1262 A. D.). He was a descendant of Uchi-maro, and son of Ari-nori, who was an official belonging to the palace of the Empress Dowager. As a boy he went to mount Hi-ei, where he studied the doctrine of the Ten-dai sect. In his twenty-ninth year, he became the disciple of Hō-nen, from whom he received the tradition of the doctrine of the Pure Land. Although there were many fellow-disciples, he was especially favoured by his teacher. Afterwards he compiled a book with the title of Kyō-gyō-shin-shō-mon-rui, or 'Collection of Maxims concerning the Doctrine, Practice, Faith and Enlightenment. In this work he showed the important meaning of the doctrine, as taught by the master. This is therefore the standard book of this sect.

II. The doctrine of the sect.

As has already been stated, the foundation of the doctrine of this sect is the Original Prayer of Amitâbha Buddha. Therefore its faith and practice have for their only object to follow the 'Other Power of the Original Prayer' (Hon-gwan-ta-riki), and to go to be born in the Pure Land of the Buddha. The Original Prayer is the eighteenth of his forty-eight prayers, which is as follows: — 'If any of living beings of the ten regions, who have believed in me with true thoughts and desire to be born in my country, and have even to ten times repeated the thought (of my name), should not be born there, then may I not obtain the perfect knowledge.'

This Original Prayer sprang from his gerat compassinate desire, which longed to deliver living beings from suffering. With this Original Prayer, he practised good actions during many kalpas, intending to bring his stock of merits to maturity for the sake of other living beings. All his actions, speeches and thoughts were always pure and true, so that he accomylished his great compasionate desire. It is also called the great and wide wisdom of Buddha. This Prayer and Practice excelled those of all other

Buddhas. The state of Buddha which is the fruit of such a cause is called Amida, or Amitâbha and Amitâyus, that is, 'Immeasurable Light' and 'Immeasurable Life. It also means the perfection and unlimitedness of wisdom and compassion. Therefore he can take hold of the faithful beings within his own light and let them go to be born in his Pure Land. This is called the 'Other Power of the Original Prayer.'

The creed of the sect is explained as the believing thought which follows the Original Prayer, and is in correspondence with the wisdom of Buddha. This is the same as the therefold faith enumerated in the Original Prayer, namely, 1. the true thought, 2. the belief, and 3. the desire to be born in the Pure Land. Though these are reckoned as three, the substance is only one, that is called the 'believing thought,' or the 'one thought.' If we examine our own heart, it is far from being pure and true, being bad and despicable, false and hypocritical. How can we cut off all our passions and reach Nirvâ*n*a by our own power! How can we also form the threefold faith! Therefore knowing the inability of our own power, we should believe simply in the vicarious Power of the Original Prayer. If we do so, we are in correspondence with the wisdom of Buddha and share his great compassion, just as the water of rivers becomes salt as soon as it enters the sea. For this reason, this is called the faith in the 'Other Power' (Tariki).

If we dwell in such a faith, our practice follows spontaneously, as we feel thankful for the favour of Buddha, remember his mercy, and repeat his name. This is the 'repetition of the thought (of Buddha's name) only ten times,' as spoken in the Original Prayer. It does, of course, not limit to the number ten, so that the words Nai-shi, or 'even to' are added. There will be some who may repeat the name of Buddha for the whole life, while walking, dwelling, sitting or lying down. Some may, however, do the Nem-butsu, or 'remembrance of Buddha' only once before they die. Whether often or not, our practice of repeating Buddha's name certainly follows our faith. This is explained as we can constantly practise Buddha's compassion, because we share the great merciful heart of Buddha. Again this Nem-butsu does not only mean to invocate Buddha's name, but the body and thought are also in correspondence with it, and not separated from the Buddha's mercy. This is not the action of the 'self power' of ignorant poople. It is therefore called the practice of the 'Other Power' (Ta-riki-no-ki-gyō).

This faith and practice are easy of attainment by any one. Accordingly the general Buddhistic rules of 'becoming homeless, and free from worldly desires, in order to attain to Buddhahood,' are not considered as essential in this sect. Consequently even the priests of the sect are allowed to marry and eat flesh and fish, while those of all other Buddhist sects are strictly prohibited from doing so.

Those who belong to this sect are recommended to keep to their occupation properly, and to discharge their duty, so as to be able to live in harmony. They should also cultivate their persons and regulate their families. They sould keep order and obey the laws of the government, and do the best for the sake of the country. Buddha says in the Great Sûtra (i. e. the larger Sukhâvatîvyûha): 'You should separate yourselves from all evil, and select and practise what is good, thinking and cansidering well.' The followers of this sect are already in correspondence with the Original Prayer of Amitâbha Buddha, so that they are also in harmony with the instruction of *S*âkyamuni, and the general teaching on morality. This is the Sa*m*v*ri*ti-satya (Zoku-tai), or truth by general consent, a part of the doctrine of this sect, which has reference to the distinction of good and evil in conduct in this world.

Now, as to the Paramârtha-satya (Shin-dai), or 'true truth,' which refers to the distinction of belief and doubt in the mind, what benefits do the believers derive by their putting faith in Buddha? In the present life, they become the members of the Samyaktva-râ*s*i (Shō-jō-ju), or 'mass of absolute truth.'

In the next life they attain to Nirvâna (Metsu-do).

In the first place, the mass of absolute truth means the class of beings who will certainly be born in the Pure Land of Amitâbha Buddha, and attain to Nirvâna there in the next life. They are taken hold of within the light of Amitâbha Buddha, joyful in heart, practising always the great compassion of Buddha, and suffer transmigration no more. Therefore they are called Avaivartikas (Fu-tai-ten), or 'those who never return again.' They derive this benefit at the moment of their putting faith in Buddha.

In the second place, to attain to Nirvâna means to join the state of enlightenment of Amitâbha Buddha, as soon as they are born in his Pure Land The cause of their going there, is to receive the great mercy and wisdom of Buddha; so that they can most assuredly attain to the state of Buddha (or Nirvâna), in which both the mercy and wisdom are full and perfect. The cause and effect are quite natural indeed. Those who belong to several schools of the Holy Path have to practise the three trainings of the higher morality, thought and learning, with their own power, and destroy all hunman passions, in order to attain to Nirvâna. Those of the other schools of the doctrine of the Pure Land are said to attain to Buddhahood, having practised good works for a long time in the Pure Land, where they are born from here. But in the True sect, the difference is explained by the term Ō-jō-soku-jō-butsu, or 'going to be born (in the Pure Land) is becoming Buddha.' That is to say, when the believers abandon the impure body of the present life (i. e. die) and are born in that Pure Land, they at once accomplish the highest and most excellent fruit of Nirvâ*n*a. This is because they simply rely upon the Other Power of the Original Prayer.

In this sect, neither spells nor supplications to Buddhas or other objects worshipped are employed for avoiding misfortunes, because misfortunes are originated either in the far causes of previous exisstences, or in those of the present life. The latter kind of causes should be carefully avoided; so that the believers in this doctrine, following Buddha's instruction, may become free from the present causes of misfortunes. But the far causes, having been originated in previous existences, cannot be stopped. As to the past, reproof is useless; but the future may be provided against. This is the reason why anything like a spell is not at all used in this sect. Moreover the principle of Buddhism is to obtain release from the state of transmigration and enter that of Nirvâ*n*a. Then, no happiness or misfortune of this world can desturb the thoughts of the believers. But when they turn their thoughts towards the good of others, the peace of the world should of course be desired by them. If so, they should do nothing but follow the instruction of Buddha *S*âkyamuni. Then there will follow ultimately such benefits as the world being harmonious, the country prosperous, and the people peaceful.

CHAPTER XII.

The Nichi-ren-shū, or Nichi-ren sect.

I. A history of the sect.

(a) The origin of the establishment of the sect.

Although *S*âkyamuni's manners of teaching are numbered by thousands of myriads, such as the Hînayâna and the Mahâ-yâna, temporary and true, apparent and hidden, subordinate and original, etc., yet his object is nothing but to lead living beings to the highest state of Nirvâ*n*a by the way of gradual teaching. Therefore, in the last period of his life, *S*âkyamuni preached the Saddharma-pu*nd*arîka-sûtra (Hoke-kyō),[1] or 'Sûtra of the Lotus of the Good Law.' In this Sûtra, he compared all the Sûtras preached in the three periods past, present and future; and called the Saddharma-pu*nd*arîka the best of all. This judgment was made by him according to the rules of preaching of all Buddhas past, present and future; so that even Mañ*g*usrî and Kâ*s*yapa dared not say a word againist it.

As *S*âkyamuni's own preaching was in this order, all the Buddhist teachers in the later periods followed that order, through the Three Periods of the Law, viz., the Period of the Right Law (Shō-bō), of the Image Law (Zō bō), and of the Latter Day Law (Mappō). During the two thousand years of the first

[1] *No.* 134.

two periods, therefore, all the great teachers promulgated the Law, either the Hîna or the Mahâ-yâna the temporary or the true, according to *S*âkyamuni's command. Now, the Period of the Latter Day of the Law came, when the original or primitive doctrine of the Saddharma-pu*nd*arîka was to be expounded. In 1252 A. D., when all the other sects had already been established, Nichi-ren, founder of the sect, began to promulgate the doctrine of the Saddharma-pu*nd*arîka only. He did so, following the rules of *S*âkyamuni's teaching, and explaining the doctrine taught by *S*âkyamuni himself. This excellent doctrine, giving benefits to the people of the present period, had never been known, during two thousand two hundred and twenty years since *S*âkyamuni entered Nirvâ*n*a. For Nichi-ren was most probably an incarnation of the Bodhisattva Visish*t*a*k*âritra (Jō-gyō, lit. 'eminent conduct'), who had been a 'primitive convert' (Hon-ke)[2] of *S*âkyamuni, and received special instruction from the latter, in the chapter on the Transcendent Power of the Tathâgata,[3] amidst the so called 'Sky

[2] For this Bodhisattva, see the 15th and 21st chapters of the Ho-ke-kyō, i. e. Kumâra*g*îva's Chinese tranlation, and also the 14th and 20th chapters of Kern's English version of the Saddharma-pu*nd*arîka, Sacred Books of the East, Vol. XXI.

[3] I. e. the 21st chapter of Kumâra*g*îva's version, and the 20th of Kern's.

Assembly' at Mount Gṛidhrakûṭa. This Bodhisattva was born in Japan under the name of Nichi-ren, at the proper time for promulgating the doctrine, which had been transmitted to him from Sâkyamuni. Thus Nichi-ren first established this sect in Japan, expecting to make his doctrine known in the world at large, during the ten thousand years of the Period of the Latter Day of the Law.

The sect is, therefore, either called Hokke-shū or 'Saddharma-puṇḍarîka-sect,' after the title of the principal Sûtra, or Nichi-ren-shū, after the name of the founder. Though this sect adopts the Saddharmapuṇḍarîka as the principal Sûtra, like the Ten-dai sect, yet the substance of the doctrine is very different from the latter; so that it is also called Nichi-ren-hokke-shū, or Nichi-ren's Saddharma-puṇḍarîka sect.

The following are the principal Sûtras and commentaries of this sect:

1. Myō-hō-ren-ge-kyō (Saddharma-puṇḍarîka-sûtra),[4] eight volumes, translated by Kumâragîva, under the Shin dynasty of the Yō family, 384–417 A. D.

2. Mu-ryō-gi-gyō (Amitârtha-sûtra),[5] translated by Dharmagâtayasas, under the Northern Sei dynasty, 479–502 A. D.

3. Kwan-fu-gen-kgō (Samantabhadra-dhyâna-sûtra),[6] translated by Dharmamitra, under the Sō

[4] *No.* 134. [5] *No.* 133. [6] *No.* 394.

dynasty, 420–479 A. D.

The second and third Sûtras are called the Introduction to and Conclusion of the first sûtra.

4. Chū-ho-ke-kyō, or 'Commentary on the Sad-dharma-pu*nd*arîka-sûtra,' ten volumes, compiled by Nichi-ren.

5. Ku-ketsu, or 'Oral Decisions,' two volumes, containing the teaching of Nichi-ren, as recorded by his chief disciple Nichi-kō.

(b) The Line of Transimission of the Law.

In Nichi-ren's Sadharma-pu*nd*arîka-sect, there are two lines of transmission of the Law, viz, internal and external. The external transmission is the line of the teachers in the three countries of India, China and Japan, who expounded the doctrine of the Sad-dharma-pundarîka, namely: —

*S*âkyamuni Buddha. Bhaisha*g*yarâ*g*a (Yaku-ō) Bodhisattva.	India.
Ten-dai Dai-shi (the 'great teacher').	China.
Den-gyō Dai-shi. Nichi-ren Dai-bo-satsu (Bodhisattva Mahâsattva).	Japan.

The internal transmisson is the line of those who understood the truth of the 'original or primitive doctrine' (Hon-mon), contained within the Stûpa of Prabhûtaratna (Ta-hō-tō), according to the chapters on the Preacher (Hosshi-hon, i. e. the 10th chapter) and the Transcendent Power of the Tathâgata (Jin-dzū-hon, i. e. Jin-riki-hon, the 20th chapter of the Sanskrit text and the 21st of the Chinese version), namely: —

*S*âkyamani Buddha.

Visish*t*a*k*âritra Bodhisattva (Jō-gyō Bosatsu).

Nichi-ren Dai-bo-satsu.

Though the outer form of the doctrine of this sect depends on that of the Ten-dai sect, the principle is absolutely in harmony with the principal Sûtra; so that the internal transmission is much more correct than the external one.

II. The Doctrine of the sect.

(a) An outline of the Saddharma-pu*nd*arîka-sûtra.

The Saddharma-pu*nd*arîka-sûtra contains the doctrine which is characterized by the term Gon-jitsu-hon-jaku-kai-e, i. e. 'open comprehension of temporary and true (doctrines), and that of original and subordinate (states of Buddha).' The 'temporary'(Gon) doctrine is that of all the Sûtras spoken by Buddha during the first forty years of his career, before he spoke the Saddharma-pu*nd*arîka-sûtra, which alone contains the 'true' (Jitsu) doctrine. The 'original' (Hon) or primitive state of Buddha means the 'original enlightenment' (Hon-gaku) of the very remote time when Buddha was in his primitive stage (Hon-ji). The 'subordinate' (Shaku, lit. footprint) or secondary state of Buddha is the 'first enlightenment' (Shi-kaku) of Buddha's life-time in this world (Sui-shaku). The 'open comprehension' (Kai-e) means to show the final truth, as the object of the appearance of *S*âkyamuni in this world.

In the first place we shall explain the 'open comprehension of the temporary and true doctrines' (Gon-jitsu-kai-e). When *S*âkyamuni appeared in this world, there were three classes of beings concerning the power of their unederstanding. The lowest class was called *S*râvakas (Shō-mon) or 'hearers;' the middle, Pratyekabuddhas (En-gaku) or 'singly enlightened;' and the highest, Bodhisattvas (Bo-satsu) or 'beings of wisdom.' Buddha taught the *S*râvakas to destroy passions, separate from transmigration, and attain to the state of Arhat (A-ra-kan). He instructed those who were capable of becoming Pratyekabuddhas, to attain to that state. The Bodhisattvas were taught to make the great vow and prayer to save all beings and bocome Buddhas like *S*âkyamuni himself, when their meritorious actions had been completed. These three classes were called Tri-yâna (San-jō) or 'three vehicles,' the first two being the Hîna-yâna (Shō-jō) or 'small vehicle,' and the last, the Mahâ-yâna (Dai-jō) or 'great vehicle.' One who attained either to the state of Arhat or Pratyekabuddha, according to the Hîna-yâna, did not become Buddha of the Mahâyâna; and vice versâ. One person could not comprehend two ways at once. They were, therefore, taught to practise any of the three vehicles at their pleaaure. So, there were three distinct classes of people, who became the sages of as many vehicles. This is called the doctrine of temporary expedient.

Thus, during the first forty years, Buddha spoke several Sûtras, observing the distinctions of three vehicles. But in the Saddharma-pu*nd*arîka, he declared that all his speeches of the first forty years were expedients, and that there was only one vehicle (Eka-yâna) and not three. Farther he said: 'The *S*râvakas and Pratyekabuddhas are also the Mahâyâna and able to become Buddhas. Even the I*kkh*antis (Is-sen-dai) or 'unfaithful men' and women are able to attain to Buddhahood. All living beings are possessed of the nature of Buddha; so that there is reason to believe that every one without exception can become enlightened. This is my true doctrine, which should not be doubted. However the temporary doctrine of expedients has been spoken by me for the purpose of leading men to the true path of the Saddharma-pu*nd*arîka. Therefore the temporary doctrine itself is true in some respects. The temporary doctrine is like the lotus flower, and the true doctrine is like the fruit or seeds of the lotus. The flower is truly the expedient for the fruit. The expedient and the truth are unseparable. No expedient exists without truth. No truth appears without expedient. They are almost one, though numbered two. This is called the Lotus of the Good Law.'

When Buddha spoke these words, the practisers of the three vehicles at once understood the truth of the one vehicle by the merits produced from their previous practice according to the temporary doctrine. So, even Devadatta and the daughter of the king of the Nâgas or serpents immediately ascended the throne of Buddha.

This is the form of preaching of the 'subordinate doctrine' (Shaku-mon) of the Saddharma-pu*nd*a-rîka, in which the 'temporary' doctrine is explained to be expedient for showing the truth, and the three vehicles are looked upon as if they were only one.

In the second place, the 'open comprehension of the original and subordinate states of Buddha' (Hon-jaku-kai-e) is explained in the following way:—

The state of Buddha to which *S*âkyamuni attained in this world through the eight stages of his life (Has-sō-jō-dō), is called Shi-jō-shō-gaku, or the 'first accomplishment of the perfect enlightenment.' The term is shortened into Shi-kaku, or the 'first enlightenment; and this is the subordinate Buddha (Shaku-butsu). The enlightenment of *S*âkyamuni here was only to perceive that he himself had been the Buddha of original enlightenment, the lord of the Dharmadhâtu (Hokkai, lit. 'element of law or existence'), since very remote times. All Buddhas of the ten regions of the three times, past, present and future, are in the same way. During the 'temporary' teaching of the first forty years, *S*âkyamuni spoke of himself as he first attained to Buddhahood in this world as it appeared to be so. But when he spoke the Saddharma-pu*nd*arîka, he manifested his real state of 'original enlightenment,' as he was the Buddha of permanency and the lord of the whole universe. But no 'original enlightenment' is manifested unless the 'first enlightenment' has been attained here, just as the flowers and the moon of the former days can be understood only after we see those of to-day. Again we can know the Buddhas of the ten regions by seeing one Buddha only, and recognise that we ourselves are already Buddhas by hearing the state of other Buddhas. All Buddhas of the subordinate state are like the images of the moon reflected upon several waters, and only the Buddha of the original state is like the real moon in the sky. The 'subordinate' state is shown by the 'original' one, and vice versâ. Though they are different from each other, their virtue is one and the same. This is called the Lotus of the Good Law.

When Buddha preached this doctrine, the whole assembly of living beings of ten different worlds, who were present in the Dai-ko-kū-e, or 'Great Sky Assembly,' upon Mount G*ri*dhrakû*t*a (Ryō–zen), attained to the state of Buddha. This is the form of preaching of the 'original doctrine' (Hon-mon) of the Saddharma-pu*nd*arîka.

In short, the character of the 'subordinate doctrine' (Shaku-mon) is to sum up all his speeches, and explain the original intention of his appearance in the world, which is to cause all men and women, whether good or bad, strong or weak in understanding, to join Buddhism. It is also to make the distinctions of several teachings even, and show the wisdom of the one vehicle of Buddha which is just and equal. But the character of the 'original doctrine' (Hon-mon) is to show the origin of all beings, and the real state of enlightenment of the Buddhas of the three times, past, present and future. It also explains that all laws are good and all beings are Buddhas.

The Bhagavat did not teach this excellent law of the original doctrine to the ordinary Bodhisattvas such as Mañ*g*usrî, Bhaisha*g*yarâ*g*a (Yaku-ō) and others. How much less did he teach it to the inferior disciples? He carefully instructed in this doctrine the Bodhisattva Visish*t*a*k*âritra (Jō-gyō) and some others who appeared on the earth. The place in which they were appointed to promulgate the law is this world Sahâ (Sha-ba) or *G*ambudvîpa; and the time is called either the Period of the Latter Day of the Law, the World of evil and corruption, or the Last 500 years. This is called the Special Instruction in the Original Doctrine of the Soddharma-pu*nd*arîka.

(b) The Three Great Secret Laws.

The important points of the doctrine of Nichi-ren's sect are called the Three Great Secret Laws or Doctrines, which include all rules of Buddhism. In the chapter on the Duration of the Life of the Tathâgata (Ju-ryō-hon) in the Saddharma-pu*nd*arîka, Buddha spoke of the permanency of the three bodies of Buddha, namely, 1. Dharma-kâya (Hosshin) or the 'spiritual body,' 2. Sa*m*bhoga-kâya (Hō-shin) or the 'body of compensation,' and 3. Nirmâ*n*a-kâya (Ō-ge-shin) or the body capable of transformation. This doctrine is the essence of the Sûtra and the object of the appearance of Buddha in the world; so that it is taken to be the substance of the Three Great Secret Laws. In the Sûtra there occurs the term 'the Tathâgata's Secret Supernatural Power' (Nyo-rai-hi-mitsu-jin-dzū-shi-riki), whence the name of the Three Great Secret Laws.

The Three Laws are the Hon-zon, Dai-moku, and Kai-dan of the Hon-mon, i. e. the chief Object of Worship, the Title of the sûtra, and the Place for learning the *S*îla or moral precepts, all of which belong to the Original Doctrine. The substance of these is contained in the title of the Sûtra which consists of the five Chinese characters, Myō-hō-ren-ge-kyō (Saddharma-pu*nd*arîka-sûtra). We remember in our mind the chief object of worship, recite with our mouth the title of the Sûtra, and keep in our body the place of

*S*îla, or simply moral precepts.

First, the chief object of worship (Hon-zon) of the Original Doctrine is the great Ma*nd*ala of the ten different worlds, which is the body of Buddha, in whom the followers of the sect believe. This Ma*nd*ala represents the original Buddha of very remote times. This Buddha's 'spiritual body' (Hosshin) consists of the five elements (Earth, Water, Fire, Wind, and Ether) of the Dharmadhâtu of ten regions. The five Skandhas or collections (Form, Perception, Name, Conception, and Knowledge) of the Dharmadhâtu of the ten regions form the nature of the 'body of compensation' (Hō-shin) of this Buddha. The six organs of sense of all beings of ten regions are the form of the 'body capable of transformation' (Ō-ge-shin) of this Buddha. The three actions (of Body, Speech, and thought) and the four dignified postures (of Going,Remaining, sitting, and Lying) of all beings are the actions of this Buddha. The wisdom and virtue of all sages and wise men of every region and the enlightenment of all Buddhas are the supernatural powers of this Buddha. All countries of every region are his dwelling-place. He is free from birth and death, even after passing through immeasurable Kalpas. He is the Buddha of permanency, without beginning and end. This Buddha is called *S*âkyamuni who truly accomplished his state of Buddha in very remote times (Ku-on-jitsu-jō), or the 'original

Buddha of three bodies that do nothing' (Mu-sa-san-jin-no-hon-butsu).

The ten worlds from the world of Buddhas down to that of hells, are all transformations of this original Buddha. The chief object of worship (Hon-zon) is the representation of this Buddha, so that the five characters of Myō-hō-ren-ge-kyō (Saddharma-pu*nd*arîka-sûtra) are written down in the middle, around which the forms of the ten worlds are added to show the nature of the original Buddha.

Now *S*âkyamuni said of himself, in the chapter on the duration of the Ṭathâgata's life, that he was really this original Buddha. But not only was *S*âkyamuni so, but even we ourselves are the same. This is the way of meditating on the chief object of worship.

Secondly, the five characters Myō-hō-ren-ge-kyō form the title of the Sûtra, so that the name of Dai-moku or 'title' is given to them. To these five characters, two more viz No-mu (Namas, or 'adoration') are added. Thus we repeat Na-mu-myō-hō-ren-ge-kyō (Nama*h* Saddharmapu*nd*arîkâya Sûtrâya), or 'adoration to the Sûtra of the Lotus of the Good Law.' This is to believe in the Good Law of the heart with the heart of the Good Law. The title of the Sûtra which consists of five characters, is the essence of the whole Sûtra as well as of the holy teaching of Buddha's whole life, the principle of all things, the truth of eternity, and the secret importance of Buddha's original state and of the virtue of his enlightenment. It is quite beyond the reach of explanation and reasoning, except in so far as one may say that it is inexplicable and inconceivable. It is not understood even by the subordinate Buddhas and the highest Bodhisattvas. How much less can it be known by the inferior beings? It is simply to be believed in, and not to be understood at all. This is the title of the original doctrine.

Thirdly, the Kai-dan, or 'place for receiving instruction in *S*îla or moral precepts,' of the original doctrine is explained as follows: To keep the *S*îla is the most important matter of all the divisions of Buddha's doctrine, whether of the great or small vehicle of the true or of the temporary. Therefore there is in the original doctrine the first true *S*îla which is held by Buddha permanently. The Kai-dan is the Bodhi-ma*nd*a (Dō-jō) or 'place for the way,' where the ceremony to receive instruction in the *S*îla is to be accomplished. The place is now mentioned instead of the law which is to be observed there.

The substance of this *S*îla is the title of the five characters Myō-hō-ren-ge-kyō. One who believes in this title and observes it, is said to be the holder of the excellent *S*îla of the original doctrine. The place where he keeps and holds it, is the Pure Land of the Calm Light (Jak-kō-jō-do), i. e. the Kai-dan.

In short one should remember that his own body is the Original Buddha (Hon-zon), thought is the Good Law (Dai-moku), and the dwelling-place is the Pure Land of Constantly Calm Light (Kai-dan). Thus he should dwell in the Dharmadhâtu, or 'spiritual state,' of his own thought.

Though the rules of practice of Buddhism are various, the three trainings (San-gaku) of the higher morality (Kai), thought (Jō) and learning (E) are the most important. By the higher morality one keeps off the bad conduct of his body; by the higher thought, he tranquilizes his mind; and by the higher learning, he becomes free from confusion and attains to enlightenment. There is no Buddhist sect which does not take these three trainings as the principle of their practice, though each sect possesses its own peculiar excellence.

So this sect is the same. The Three Great Secret Laws are the three trainings of the sect. The Kai-dan is of course the morality (Kai). The meditation or thought (Jō) is to believe in the chief object of worship (Hon-zon) and to meditate on the Good Law. The learning (E) is to repeat the title of the Sûtra (Dai-moku), which contains the wisdom of all Buddhas, and to show the excellence of the wisdom.

If one keeps these Three Secret Laws, the three

trainings are quickly accomplished, and immeasurable Samâdhis (San-mai) or meditations and Pâramitâs (Ha-ra-mitsu) or perfections of practice are spontaneously completed. Therefore even a being of weak understanding can enter on the precions rank of the enlightened in his present life. Thus the doctrine of this sect is very deep and wonderful indeed.

Sanskrit-Chinese Index.

Akusala-mahâbhûmika-dharma, 8	大不善地法
Akshobhya, 92	阿閦
Aṅguttara-nikâya (Pâli), 35	增一阿含
A*g*âtasatru, 105	阿闍世
A*g*ita, 73	阿逸多
A*tat*a, IX	頞哳陀
Advesha, 7	無瞋
Adhi*k*itta, 109	定(三學之一)
Adhipra*gñ*â, 109	慧(同)
Adhimoksha, 7	勝解
Adhi*s*îla, 109	戒(三學之一)
Anapatrapâ, 8	無愧
Anavatapta, 52	阿耨達(池)
Anâgâmin, 109	阿那含
Anâthapi*nd*ada, XVII	給孤獨
Anityatâ, 10	滅
Aniyata-bhûmika-dharma, 9	不定地法
Apatrapâ, 7	愧
Apapa, IX	臛々婆
Apratisa*m*khyâ-nirodha, 10	非擇滅
Apramâda, 7	不放逸
Aprâpti, 9	非得
Abhidharma, 16	阿毗達磨
Abhidharma-ko*s*a-*s*âstra, 1	阿毗達磨俱舍論
Abhidharma-pi*t*aka, 2	阿毗達磨藏

Abhinishkrama*n*a-sûtra XV 本起經

Abhisheka, 75 灌頂

Amitâbha, 93 阿彌陀(無量光)

Amitâyur-dhyâna-sûtra, 105 觀無量壽經

Amitâyus, 126 阿彌陀(無量壽)

Amitâyus-sûtra, 104 阿彌陀經

Amitârtha-sûtra, 134 無量義經

Amoghava*g*ra, 75,79,81 不空金剛

Amoghasiddhi, 93 不空成就

Ayodhya, 32 阿踰闍

Arûpa, 37 無色

Arbuda, IX 頞部陀

Arhat, 3,26,110,137 阿羅漢

Alobha, 7 無貪

Avata*m*saka, 52,71 華嚴

Avata*m*saka-sûtra, 22,32 華嚴經

Avalokite*s*vara, 90,97 觀世音(觀自在)

Avalokite*s*vara-v*ri*ti, 96,98 觀音院

Avi*gñ*apti-rûpa, 5 無表色

Avidyâ, 85 無明

Avî*k*i, IX 阿鼻(無間)

Avaivartika, 129 不退轉

A*s*râddhya, 8 不信

A*s*vaghosha, 52, 53,59,106,115 馬鳴

Ash*t*apattra-v*ri*ti, 97 八葉院

Asa*m*khya, 11,42,62,57 阿僧祇耶(無數)

Asa*m*ga, 32 無著

Asa*mgñ*ika, 9 無想果

Asa*mgñ*i-samâpatti, 9 無想定
Asa*m*skr*i*ta, 4,87 無為
Asa*m*skr*i*ta-dharma, 10,38,40 無為法
Astika, 47,48,49 有見(有執)
Asura, 61 阿修羅
Ahi*m*sâ, 7 不害
Ahrîkatâ, 8 無慚

Âkâ*s*a, 10,11 虛空
Âkâ*s*agarbha-v*r*iti,96,98 虛空藏院
Âgama, 35,71 阿含
Â*k*ârya, 75,77 阿闍梨
Âtman, 12,14,15,16,35 我
Âdar*s*ana-*gñ*âna, 100 大圓鏡智
Ânanda, 26,115 阿難陀
Âyatana, 4 處
Âlaya-vi*gñ*âna, 39 阿賴耶識

I*kkh*anti, 138 一闡提
Indriya, 5 根

Îrshyâ, 8 嫉

Utpala, IX 嗢鉢羅
Upakle*s*a-bhûmika-dharma, 8 小煩惱地法
Upagupta, 26, 53, 115 優婆毱多
Upanâha, 8 恨
Upâdhyâya, 28, 73 和上

Upâli, 21, 26 優波離
Upekshâ, 7 捨
Uruvilvâ-kâsyapa, XIV 優樓頻螺迦葉

Eka-mudrâ-parshad, 91, 95. 一印會
Ekayâna, 66, 138 一乘
Ekavyavahârika, 52 一說部
Ekottarâgama, 35 增一阿含

Auddhatya, 8 掉舉

Kapimala, 116 迦毗摩羅
Kapilavastu, XII, XV 迦毗羅衛
Karma, 11, 90, 91 羯磨(業)
Karman, 21, 25, 28 羯磨
Karma-parshad, 91, 96 羯磨會
Karma-ma*nd*ala, 90, 94 業曼荼羅
Karma-va*k*ana, 25 羯磨文
Karma-va*g*ra, 93 羯磨波羅[illegible]
Karmânubhâva, 90 羯磨部
Kalpa, 11, 62, 67, 104 劫波
Kâ*n*adeva, 116 迦那提婆
Kâtyâyana, 2 迦旃延
Kâma, 36 欲
Kâya, 5 身
Kâya-vi*g*ñâna, 6, 38 身識
Kâlayas*a*s, 105 畺良耶舍
Kâlasûtra, IX 黑繩

Kâlya, XIV 迦陵
Kâ*s*yapa, 115 迦葉
Kâ*s*yapîya, 27 迦葉毗部
Kâshi, 116 香至
Kinnara, X 緊那羅
Kinnara-râ*g*a Druma, XV 純眞陀羅王
Kumâra*g*îva, 14, 17, 45, 73,104 鳩摩羅什
Kumârata, 116 鳩摩羅多
Kumârila-bha*tt*a, 13 俱摩羅陀
Ku*s*ala-mahâbhûmika-dharma, 7 大善地法
Ku*s*alasa*m*grâha-*s*îla, 70 攝善法戒
Kushi, XVIII 拘尸(那城)
K*ri*tyânush*th*âna-*gñ*âna,100 成所作智
Kauk*ri*tya, 9 惡作
Kau*nd*inya, XIV 憍陳如
Kausîdya, 8 懈怠
Krodha, 8 忿
Klish*t*amano-vi*gñ*âna, 38 染汚意識
Kle*s*a-mahâbhûmika-dharma, 7 大煩惱地法
Kle*s*âvara*n*a, 43 煩惱障
Ksha*n*a, 15 刹那
Kshatriya, 50 刹帝利
Kshânti, 12 羼提(忍辱)
Kshitigarbha-v*ri*ti, 96,98 地藏院

Ga*g*asîrsha, XIV 象頭

Gandha, 5 香

Gandharva, X 乾闥婆

Garu*d*a, X 迦樓羅

Garbha-dhâtu, 78,79,88,89,-90,96,99,102 胎藏界

G*ri*dhrakû*t*a, 74,114,140 耆闍崛(山)

Godhanya, XV 瞿耶尼

Gomukha, 53 牛口

Grantha, 32 本頌

Ghrâ*n*a, 4 鼻

Ghrâ*n*a-vi*g*ñâna, 6,38 鼻識

*K*akshur-vi*g*ñâna, 6,38 眼識

*K*akshus, 4 眼

*K*atur-mudrâ-parshad, 81,94 四印會

*K*andâla, 50 旃陀羅

*K*itta, 5,38 心

*K*itta-râ*g*a, 38,40 心王

*K*itta viprayukta-dharma, 38,40 心不相應法

*K*itta-viprayukta-sa*m*skâra, 9 心不相應行

*K*intâmani, XIX 如意寶珠(摩尼)

*K*etanâ, 7 思

*K*aitta-dharma, 5,38,40 心所有法

*Kh*anda, 7 欲

*G*ambu-dvîpa, 57,141 閻浮提
*G*ayata, 116 闍夜多
*G*arâ, 10 異
*G*âti, 10 生
*G*ihvâ, 4 舌
*G*ihvâ-vi*gñ*âna, 6,38 舌識
*G*îvita, 10 命根
*G*eta, XIV,XV 祇陀
*G*eta-vana Anâthapi*ndad*ada-ârâma, XIV 祇樹給孤獨園
*G*eta-vana-vihâra, 29 祇園精舍
*Gñ*ânaprabha, 46 智光
*Gñ*ânaprasthâna-sâstra, 2 發智論
*Gñ*eyâvara*n*a, 43 所知障

Tathâgata, 13,23,26,32,35, 49,53,65,78,80,87,89,104,142 如來
Tathâgata-garbha, 65 如來藏
Tathâgatânubhâva, 89 佛部
Tapana, IX 焦熱
Tiryag-yoni-gata, VIII 畜生道(傍生趣)
Tiryag-yoni-sattva, 83 傍生有情
Tushita, 32 兜率(天)
Te*g*odhara-v*ri*ti, 96 持明院
Trayastri*m*sa, XVIII 忉利(天)
Tripi*t*aka, 2,13,14,20,26,49,51, 52,80,85,104,108 三藏
Triyâna, 137 三乘

Trividha-*s*îla, 69 三聚淨戒
Trailokya-vi*g*aya-parshad, 91, 95 降三世羯磨會
Trailokya-vi*g*aya-samaya-parshad, 91,95 降三世三昧耶會

Da*s*abhûmi, XIII 十地
Da*s*abhûmi-vibhâshâ-*s*âstra,59 十住毗婆沙論
Dâna-pâramitâ, 12 檀那波羅蜜多(施度)
Divâkara, 46 日照
Divyadundubhimeghanirghosha, 97 天鼓雷音
Dîgha-nikâya (Pâli), 35 長阿含
Dîrghâgama, 35 同前
Deva, 25,45,47,54,55 天
Devadatta, 139 提婆達多
Devapâla, XIV 提謂波利
Deva*s*arman, 3 提婆設摩
Devî, XII 王后(夫人)
Dvâda*s*a-nikâya (or mukha)-*s*âstra, 44,48 十二門論

Dharma, 4,10,14,15,16,21,23, 32,35,36,38,40,41,65,70 法
Dharma-kâya, 63,69,78,82, 110,142 法身
Dharmakâla, 27 法時
Dharmagupta, 13,20,21,26,27 曇無德

Dharmagupta-vinaya, 22,23 四分律
Dharmagâtayasas, 134, 曇摩伽陀耶舍
Dharmadhâtu, 22,30,101,143 法界
Dharmadhâtu-prakriti-gñâna, 99 法界體性智
Dharmadhâtu-mandala, 83 法界曼荼羅
Dharmadhâtvavatâra, 58 入法界
Dharmapâla, 33 護法
Dharma-mandala, 90,94 法曼荼羅
Dharmamitra, 134 曇摩蜜多
Dharmalakshana, 32 法相
Dharmavagra, 93 法波羅蜜
Dharma-skandha-pâda, 2 法蘊足論
Dhâtu, 4,88 界
Dhâtu-kâya-pâda, 3 界身足論
Dhâranî, 57,62 陀羅尼
Dhritaka, 115 提多迦
Dhyâna, 12,20,114 禪那
Dhyâna-gokara, X 四禪天

Namas, 144 南無
Namah Saddharmapundarîkâya Sûtrâya, 144 南無妙法蓮華經
Namo 'mitâbhâya Buddhâya, 106 南無阿彌陀佛
Nâga, 139 龍
Nâgabodhi, 79,81 龍智
Nâgarâga, XIV 龍王

Nâgâr*g*una, 45,47,48,49,52,53,54,57, 59,74,79,80,81,106,116,124 龍樹(龍猛)
Nâmakâya, 10 名身
Nâraka, 83 捺羅迦(地獄之有情)
Nâlanda, 33 那爛陀(寺)
Nâstika, 47,48,49 無見(空執)
Nirarbuda, IX 尼剌部陀
Nirodha, 11,16 滅
Nirodha-samâpatti, 10 滅盡定
Nirmâ*n*a-kâya, 70,142 化身
Nirvâ*n*a, 11,12,21,2ff,47,49,51, 52,71,80,93,115,126,129 涅槃(滅度)
Nirvâ*n*a-sûtra, XVIII,XX 涅槃經
Nîlanetra, 45,46 青目
Nîlapadmanetra, 53 青蓮華眼
Nyâyânusâra-*s*âstra, XXI 順正理論

Padakâya, 10 句身
Padma, IX,89,90 鉢特摩(蓮華)
Padmânubhâva, 89 蓮華部
Paratantra-laksha*n*a, 36 依他起性
Paranirmita-vasa-vartin,XVII 他化自在天
Paramârtha, 3 真諦
Paramârtha-satya, 128 勝義諦
Parikalpita-laksha*n*a, 36 遍計所執性
Parinirvâ*n*a, 43 般涅槃
Parinishpanna-laksha*n*a, 36 圓成實性
Pâramitâ, 11,70,105,147 波羅蜜多

Pâr*s*va, 115 婆栗濕縛
Pindola, 25 賓頭盧
Pu*n*yamitra, 116 不如蜜多
Pu*n*yaya*s*as, 115 富那夜奢
Pushya, XV 弗迦沙
Pû*g*â-parshad, 91 供養會
Prakara*n*a-pâda, 3 品類足論
Pra*gñ*a, 58 般若(三藏)
Pra*gñ*apti-pâda, 3 施設足論
Pra*gñ*â, 12,42,110 般若
Pra*gñ*âtara, 116 般若多羅
Pra*gñ*â-pâramitâ, 52,71 般若波羅蜜多
Pra*gñ*â pâramitâ-sûtra, XVI 般若波羅蜜多經
Pra*gñ*â-sûtra, 65 般若經
Pratâpana, IX 大焦熱
Pratigha, 9 瞋
Pratisa*m*khyâ-nirodha, 10 擇滅
Pratîtyasamutpâda, 4 緣起
Pratyutpanna-buddha-sa*m*mu-
khâvasthita-sûtra, XV 般舟經
Pradâ*s*a, 8 惱
Prabhûtaratna, 29,135 多寶
Pramâda, 8 放逸
Pramuditâ-bhûmi, 49 歡喜地
Pratyaveksha*n*a-*gñ*âna, 100 妙觀察智
Pratyekabuddha, 11,51,85,137 緣覺(獨覺)
Pra*s*rabdhi, 7 輕安
Prâpta, 9 得

Preta, 51,83	餓鬼
Bahu*s*rutika, 1352	多聞部
Bahu*s*rutika-vibha*g*ya, 52	多聞分別部
Bimbisâra, 105	頻婆娑羅
Buddha, 1, etc.	佛陀(覺者)
Buddha-dhyâna-samâdhi-sâgara-sûtra, XV	觀佛三昧海經
Buddhanandi, 115	佛陀難提
Buddhabhadra, 57	覺賢
Buddhamitra, 115	伏駄蜜多
Buddhaya*s*as, 27	佛陀耶舍
Buddhâvata*m*saka-mahâvaipulya-sûtra, 62,87	大方廣佛華嚴經
Buddhigati-parshad, 91,95	理趣會
Bodhi, 42	菩提
Bodhidharma, 115,116,117	菩提達磨
Bodhima*nd*a, 145	道場
Bodhisattva, 11,etc.	菩薩(覺有情)
Bodhyaṅga, 91	菩提分(覺支)
Brahma*g*âla-sûtra, 25	梵網經
Brahman, 115	梵天
Brâhma*n*a, 50,117	婆羅門
Bhagavat, 80,114	世尊(具福智者)
Bhavaviveka, 46	清辯
Bhikshu, 25,49,53	比丘
Bhikshu*n*î, XV	比丘尼
Bhûtatathatâ, 65	眞如

Bhaisha*g*yarâ*g*a, 135,141 藥王

Magadha, 33,51,105 摩揭陀
Ma*k*ilinda, XIV 文鱗
Ma*ggh*ima-nikâya (Pâli), 35 中阿含
Ma*ñg*usrî, 51,63,97,107,132, 141 文殊師利
Ma*ñg*usrî-v*ri*ti, 96,98 文殊院
Ma*nd*ala, 78,88,90,91,94,96, 102,103,143 曼荼羅
Mati, 7 慧
Mada, 9 憍
Madhyamaka-*s*âstra, 44,47,48 中論
Madhyamâgama, 35 中阿含
Madhyamika, 44 中論派
Madhyântika, 26 末田地
Madhyânta-vibhâga-*s*âstra, 32 辯中邊論
Manas, 5 意
Manaskara, 7 作意
Manu, 50 摩拏(法律書)
Manura, 116 摩拏羅
Mano-râ*g*a, 6 心王
Mano-vi*gñ*âna, 6,38 意識
Mantra, 79,90 眞言
Marî*k*i, X 摩利支
Mahâkâ*s*yapa, 26,49,52,115 摩訶迦葉
Mahâkrodhakâya, 95 大忿怒身
Mahâ*k*intya-*s*âstra, 59 大不思議論

Mahâpadma, IX 摩訶鉢特摩
Mahâparinirvâ*n*a, 22 大般涅槃
Mahâparinirvâ*n*a-sûtra, 22 涅槃經
Mahâpû*g*â-parshad, 94 大供養會
Mahâpra*g*âpatî, XV 摩訶波闍波提
Mahâpra*g**ñ*â-pâramitâ-*s*âstra, 21 大智度論
Mahâpra*g**ñ*â-pâramitâ-sûtra, 36 大般若經
Mahâbrahman, 114 大梵天
Mahâbrahmarâ*g*a-pari*p*ri*kkh*â-sûtra, XX 大梵王問佛決疑經
Mahâbhûta, 99 大
Mahâbhûmika-dharma, 6 大地法
Mahâma*nd*ala, 90 大曼荼羅
Mahâmati, 49 大慧
Mahâmaudgalyâyana, 2,62,64 大目揵連
Mahâyâna, 14,etc. 大乘
Mahâyâna-vinaya, 25 大乘律
Mahâyâna-*s*raddhotpâda-*s*âstra, 56,66 大乘起信論
Mahâyâna-sûtra, 49,51,105 大乘經
Mahâyânâla*m*kâra-*s*âstra, 32 大乘莊嚴論
Mhârâ*g*a, XII 大王
Mahâraurava, IX 大叫喚
Mahâvibhâshâ-*s*âstra, 3 大毗婆沙論
Mahâ-v*ri*ti, 96 大院
Mahâvaipulya, 63 大方等
Mahâvaipulya-mahâsa*m*nipâta-

sûtra, XIV 大方等大集經
Mahâvairo*k*âna, 78,80,81,79,92, 94,95,97 大日
Mahâvairo*k*anâbhisa*m*bodhi-sûtra, 78 大日經
Mahâsa*m*ghika, 27,51 大衆部
Mahâsa*m*ghika-vinaya, 27 摩訶僧祇律
Mahâsattva, 135 摩訶薩(大士)
Mahîsâsaka, 13,27 彌沙塞部
Mahes*v*ara, X 大自在(天)
Mahoraga, X 摩睺羅伽
Mâtsarya, 8 嫉
Mâna, 9 慢
Mâyâ, 9 諂
Mâyâ-sûtra, 53 摩耶經
Mi*kkh*aka, 115 彌遮迦
Middha, 9 睡眠
Muktapushpa, 97 開敷華
Mudrâ, 92,94,101 印
M*ri*gadâva, XVI 鹿苑
Maitreya, 32,31,73,97 彌勒(慈氏)
Moksha, 110 解脫
Moha, 8 無明
Mraksha, 8 覆

Yaksha, X,XIV 夜叉
Yasas, XIV 耶舍
Yasodharâ, XII 耶輸陀羅

Yâna, 11,16,22,49,54,72 乘

Yoga, 32,33,72,76;77,79,86,100, 101,102 瑜伽

Yoga-*s*âstra, 41 瑜伽師地論

Yogâ*k*ârya-bhûmi-*s*âstra, 32, 65 瑜伽論

Yo*g*ana, 64 由旬

Ratna, 90 寶

Ratnadeva, 53 寶天

Ratnadhvaga, 97 寶幢

Ratnava*g*ra, 53 寶波羅蜜

Ratnasa*m*bhava, 52 寶生

Ratnânubhâva, 90 寶部

Rasa, 5 味

Râkshasa, X 羅刹

Râ*g*agr*i*ha, 9,51 王舍(城)

Râhu, X 羅睺

Râhula, 45 羅睺羅

Râhulata, 116 羅睺羅多

Rûpa, 4,5,21,36,85 色

Rûpadharma, 38,40 色法

Raurava, IX 叫喚

Laksha*n*a, 37 性

Lañkâ, XVI 楞伽

Lañkâvatâra, 49 入楞伽

Lañkâvatâra-sûtra, 48,66 入楞伽經

Lokottaravâda, 52	說出世部
Va*g*ra, 79,88,89,102	金剛
Va*g*rakarma, 93	金剛業
Va*g*raketu, 93	金剛幢
Va*g*ragandhi, 93	金剛塗香
Va*g*ragîti, 93	金剛歌
Va*g*ragha*nt*â, 94	金剛鈴
Va*g*ra*kkh*edikâ-pra*g*ñâpâramitâ-*s*âstra, 32	金剛般若論
Va*g*ratîksh*n*a, 93	金剛利
Va*g*rate*g*as, 98	金剛光
Va*g*radharma, 93	金剛法
Va*g*ra-dhâtu, 18,88,89,90,91, 96,99,102	金剛界
Va*g*radhûpa, 93	金剛香
Va*g*ran*ri*ti, 93	金剛舞
Va*g*rapâ*n*i-v*ri*ti, 96,98	金剛手院
Va*g*rapushpa, 93	金剛華
Va*g*rabandha, 92	金剛索
Va*g*rabodhi, 75,79,81	金剛智(三藏)
Va*g*ramâli, 93	金剛鬘
Va*g*rayaksha, 93	金剛牙
Va*g*raraksha, 93	金剛護
Va*g*raratna, 93	金剛寶
Va*g*rarâga, 93	金剛愛
Va*g*rarâ*g*a, 93	金剛王
Va*g*ralâsa, 93	金剛嬉

Va*g*ravâ*k*, 93 金剛語

Va*g*ra*s*ekhara-sûtra, 93 金剛頂經

Va*g*rasattva, 75,78,79,80,81, 89,93,99 金剛薩埵

Va*g*rasandhi, 93 金剛拳

Va*g*rasâdhu, 93 金剛喜

Va*g*rasphota, 94 金剛鎖

Va*g*rahâsa, 93 金剛笑

Va*g*rahetu, 93 金剛因

Va*g*rânku*s*a, 93 金剛鉤

Va*g*rânubhâva, 89 金剛部

Va*g*rânubhâva-v*ri*ti, 96,98 金剛院

Va*g*râloka, 93 金剛燈

Va*s*asuta, 116 婆舍斯多

Vasubandhu, 32,33,106,116, 124 天親(世親)

Vasumitra, 3,119 世友

Vârâ*n*asî, XIV 波羅奈

Vâstîputrîya, 27 婆麤富羅

Vi*k*âra, 9 思

Vi*k*ikitsâ, 9 疑

Vi*gñ*âna, 5,37,65,85,99 識

Vi*gñ*âna-kâya-pâda, 3 識身足論

Vitarka, 9 尋

Vidyâmâtra, 32,33 唯識

Vidyâmâtra-siddhi-*s*âstra, 38, 41 成唯識論

Vidyâmatra-siddhi-*s*âstra-

kârikâ, 38 唯識三十頌
Vinaya, 14,20, etc. 毗奈耶(律)
Vinaya-pi*t*aka, 26 毗奈耶藏
Vibhaga-yoga-*s*âstra, 32 分別瑜伽論
Vimalakîrtti-nirde*s*a, 18,52 維摩經
Vîmalakîrtti-nirde*s*a-sûtra, XVI 同
Vi*s*ish*t*a*k*âritra, 133,136,141 上行
Vi*s*esha*k*inta-brahma-pari*p*ri*kkh*â-sûtra, XVI 思益梵天所問經
Vi*s*vakarman, X 毗首羯磨
Vishaya, 5 境
Vihi*m*sa, 8 害
Vî*g*a, 90 種字
Vîrya, 7,12 勤(精進)
Ve*n*uvana, XIV,XVII 竹林
Vedanâ, 6,85 受
Vaidehî, 105 韋提希
Vaipulya, 71 方等
Vairo*k*ana, 29,63,69,72,73,75 毗盧遮那(大日)
Vai*s*âli, XIV,XVI,XVIII 毗舍離
Vai*s*ya, 50 吠舍
Vai*s*rama*n*a, 25 毗沙門(多聞)
Vyañ*g*anakâya, 10 文身

*S*akra Devânâm Indra, X 釋提桓因
*S*a*n*avâsa, 26,115 商那和修
*S*ata*s*âstra, 44,54,55 百論

*S*abda, 5 聲
*S*abda-vidyâ, 33 聲明
*S*âkya, 45 釋迦
*S*âkyamuni, 21, etc. 釋迦牟尼
*S*âkya-v*ri*ti, 96,98 釋迦院
*S*â*th*ya, 9 誑
*S*âriputra, 2,62,64 舍利弗
*S*âla, XVIII 娑娑
*S*âstra, 1,12, etc. 論
*S*ik*sh*â, 109 學
*S*ik*sh*ânanda, 58 實叉難陀
*S*îla, 12,21,24, stc. 尸羅(戒)
*S*îlananda, 53 尸羅難陀
*S*îla-pâramitâ, 21,29 尸羅波羅蜜多(戒度)
*S*îlabhadra, 33 戒賢
*S*uddhodana, XII,XV 淨飯
*S*ubhakarasi*m*ha, 75,81 善無畏
*S*ûdra, 50 首陀羅
*S*ûra*m*gama-samâdhi-sûtra,
XVI 首楞嚴三昧經
*S*raddhâ, 7 信
*S*rama*n*a, 52 沙門
*S*râvaka, 11,16,51,62,64,85,
137 聲聞
*S*râvastî, XIV,XVII 舍衛
*S*rîmâlâ, 18 勝鬘
*S*rîmâlâ-devî-si*m*hanâda, 52 勝鬘經
*S*rîmâlâ-devî-si*m*hanâda-sûtra,

XVI 同
*S*rîmâlâ-sûtra, 21,42 同
*S*resh*th*in, XIV 長者
*S*rotra, 4 耳
*S*rotra-vi*g*ñâna, 6,28 耳識

Sha*t*-pâda, 2 六足
Sha*n*-mahâbhûta, 99 六大

Sa*m*yuktâgama, 35 雜阿含
Sa*m*yutta-nikâya (Pâli), 35 同
Sa*m*v*ri*ti-satya, 128 世俗諦
Sa*m*skâra, 85 行
Sa*m*sk*ri*ta, 4 無爲
Sa*m*sk*ri*ta-dharma, 40 無爲法
Sak*ri*dâgâmin, 109 斯陀含(一來)
Sa*m*gîti-paryâya-pâda, 2 集異門足論
Sa*m*gha, 21,55 僧伽
Sa*m*ghâta, IX 衆合
Sa*m*ghanandi, 116 僧伽難提
Sa*m*ghabhadra, XXI 衆賢
Sa*m*ghaya*s*as, 116 僧伽耶舍
Sa*m*ghavarman, 104 僧鎧
Sa*m**g*îva, IX 等活
Sa*m**g*ñâ, 6,85 想
Sattvava*g*ra, 93 金剛波羅蜜
Sattvârthakriyâ-*s*îla, 70 攝衆生戒
Satya, 4,16,105 諦

Satya-siddhi-*s*âstra, 13,14,15, 17 成實論
Saddharma-pu*nd*arîka, 18,22, 71,74 妙法蓮華經
Saddharma-pu*nd*arîka-sûtra, 22,44,67,122, etc. 同
Sa*m*dhinirmo*k*ana-sûtra, 32, 35,36,37,65 解深密經
Saptapar*n*a, 49 七葉
Sabhâgatâ, 9 同分
Samatâ-*g*ñâna, 100 平等性智
Samaya, 84,95 三昧耶
Samaya-parshad, 91,94 三昧耶會
Samaya-ma*nd*ala, 90,94 三昧耶曼荼羅
Samantabhadra, 63,97 普賢
Samantabhadra-dhyâna-sûtra, 134 觀普賢經
Samantabhadra-bodhisattva-*k*aryâ-dharma-sûtra, XVIII 普賢菩薩行法經
Samâdhi, 7,20,147 三摩地
Samyaktva-râ*s*i, 128 正定聚
Sa*m*bhâra-*s*îla, 69,70 攝律儀戒
Sa*m*bhoga-kâya, 70,142 報身
Sarva*g*ña-v*ri*ti, 96,98 遍知院
Sarvanivâra*n*a-vishkambhi-v*ri*ti, 96,98 除蓋障院
Sarvâstivâda, 13,15,21,27 一切有部
Sarvâstivâdin, 1,12 同

Sahâ, 105,112,113,141 娑婆
Sâgaramudrâ-samâdhi, 61 海印三昧
Siddha, 76 悉曇(成就)
Siddhi, 72,77 悉地
Si*m*ha, 116 師子
Sukhâvatî, 49,104,105,106,113,
122,123 蘇摩提(極樂)
Sukhâvatîvyûha, 123,128 無量壽經阿彌陀經
Sukhâvatîvyûha-sûtra, XVIII 同
Sudatta, XIV 須達(善施)
Sumeru, XV 須彌(山)
Suvar*n*a-prabhâsa, 52 金光明經
Suvar*n*a-prabhâsa-sûtra, XVI 同
Susiddhi-v*ri*ti, 96,98 蘇悉地院
Sûk*s*hma-parshad, 91,94 微細會
Sûtra, 18,22,32, etc. 修多羅(經)
Sûtrâla*m*kâra-*s*âstra, 32 大莊嚴論
Sûrya, X 蘇利耶
Sûryasoma, 45 須利耶蘇摩
Soma, X 蘇摩
Sautrântika, 2,13 經部
Skandha, 4,10,16,85,143 蘊
Stûpa, 135 塔
Styâna, 8 昏沈
Sthavira, 51 上座
Sthiti, 10 住
Sparsa, 57 觸
Sm*ri*ti, 7 念

Srota-âpanna, 109 須陀洹(預流)

Haklenayasas, 116 鶴勒那
Harivarman, 13 訶梨跋摩
Hâhâdhara, IX 虎虎婆
Himâlaya, 52 雪山
Hînayâna, 1,13, etc. 小乘
Hînayâna-vinaya, 25 小乘律
Hînayâna-sûtra, 53 小乘經
H*ri*daya, 97 心
Hetu-vidyâ, 33 因明
Hrî, 7 慚

CORRECTIONS.

Page	Line	
2	25	for '*sâstra*' read 'pâda'
10	8	for 'deat a' read 'death'
13	18	for 'ohers' read 'others'
18	7	for 'Ho-ssō read 'Hossō
21	15	for 'Gō-sho' read 'Gossho'
27	13	for 'Mahâsa*m*ghîka read 'Mahasa*m*-ghika'
28	6	for 'Dō-kō' read 'Dō-gō'
"	20	for 'Gō-shū read 'Yō-shū'
30	21	'the *S*îla-at' to be left out.
37	9	for 'systems' read 'manners'
43	2	for 'Klesa-' read 'Klesa-'
45	2	for 'system...is' read 'manners...are
46	6	for the second 'Sō-rō' read 'Sō-sen'
"	26	for 'Af ter' read 'After'
52	11	for 'Ekavyahârika' read 'Ekavyava-hârika'
55	8	for 'Swore' read 'swore'
65	26	for 'Suddhas' read 'Buddhas'
72	24	for 'Fina-lly' read 'Final-ly'
86	14	for 'chin' read 'shin'
94	15	for 'Dai-ku-jō-e' read 'Dai-ku-yō-e'
105	6	for 'Amitâyus-' read 'Amitâyur-'

發兌元　佛教書英譯出版舍
東京々橋區南佐柄木町五番地

出版人　佐野正道
大坂府平民
仝京橋區南佐柄木町五番地

著譯者　南條文雄
福井縣平民
東京淺草永住町四十七番地

明治十九年九月廿五日版權免許
同　年十二月　出版

賣捌所

仝　日本橋通壹丁目　北畠茂兵衛

仝　本所外手町三十九番地　新報社

仝　麻布日ヶ窪町　鴻盟社

仝　三十間堀一丁目　明教社

仝　京橋銀坐四丁目　博聞社

仝　日本橋通り三丁目　丸善書店

仝　本町四丁目
岡島眞七

大坂備後町四丁目
博聞分社

仝　西六條花屋町
永田調兵衛

西京東六條中珠數屋
西村七郎兵衛